CONTEMPORARY
LANDSCAPE ARCHITECTURE

daab

Introduction

INTRODUCTION

Gilbert Laing Meason first coined the term landscape architecture in *Landscape Architecture of the Great Painters of Italy* (London, 1828), defining it as a discipline that encompasses design, planning, management and land preservation and restoration. This classification allows the landscape architect –whose task is sometimes being "occupied" by architects themselves– to shape the terrain and the space around an already existing architectural piece or a developing urban or regional project.

As a result of this, the landscape architect serves as a painter or sculptor who tends to offer the most poetic transcription of the language associated with a given architectural calculation. The animated (plants, trees, water, climate) and inanimate (pavement, surfaces, furniture) physical supports these professionals work with come from a geographical and social (urban, suburban and rural) context, in addition to some technical and economical conditions; their imagination provides the rest to find a creative, competent and playful solution.

The aims of landscape architecture are often at the mercy of an already established urban development. In certain instances their job lies in protecting the environment or historical patrimony, or is merely an artistic statement by exhibitionist cities with the will and resources to do so. In any case, however, the design of public spaces should meet their main objective: to satisfy the demands of its social, contemplative and recreational uses.

The fifty projects presented here primarily show the designs of new spaces and the successful restoration of others which had previously had completely different uses (industrial center, quarry, loading bay or even a penitentiary center).

Garden design, which wasn't the aim of this collection, is only presented in a more or less evident way as elements in some interior patios of condominiums, work places and parks; the bulk of the selection consists of medium size spaces that are far from the city center, built as consubstantial elements in an urban periphery development project.

Die Landschaftsarchitektur, wie sie zum ersten Mal von Gilbert Laing Meason in seinem Werk „Landscape Architecture of the Great Painters of Italy" (London, 1828) definiert wurde, ist eine Disziplin, die die Gestaltung, Planung, Verwaltung, den Schutz und die Wiederherstellung der Landschaft in sich vereint. Der Landschaftsarchitekt, dessen Aufgabe manchmal von den Architekten selbst übernommen wird, gestaltet das Gelände und den Raum, der ein bereits existierendes architektonisches Werk umgibt, bisweilen setzt er auch einen städtischen oder regionalen Landschaftsentwicklungsplan um.

So wandelt der Landschaftsarchitekt – ebenso wie ein Maler oder Bildhauer – sehr oft die architektonischen Berechnungen in eine poetischere Sprache um. Die lebenden physischen Mittel (Pflanze, Baum, Wasser, Klima) und die unbelebten (Pflaster, Fläche, Mobiliar), mit denen der Landschaftsplaner arbeitet, gehen jeweils von einem bestimmten geografischen und sozialen Kontext (Stadt, Vorstadt, Land) sowie technischen und ökonomischen Bedingungen aus. Basierend auf diesen Grundlagen ist es die Vorstellungskraft des Landschaftsarchitekten, die eine kreative, gekonnte und spielerische Lösung finden soll.

Die Ziele der Landschaftsplanung werden oft durch eine städtische Entwicklung beeinflusst, die bereits stattgefunden hat. Unter bestimmten Umständen konzentrieren sich die Landschaftsarchitekten auf den Schutz der Umwelt oder des historischen Erbes; in anderen Fällen stellen sie eine Art künstlerisches Plädoyer für exhibitionistische Städte dar, die entsprechende Mittel und die Bereitschaft haben, die Pläne umzusetzen. In all diesen Ausrichtungen sollte die Gestaltung des öffentlichen Raums jedoch stets ihrem Hauptzweck dienen, sie sollte der Nachfrage nach öffentlichem Raum nachkommen, der sozialen Zwecken, der Meditation und der Entspannung dienen.

Die etwa fünfzig Projekte, die dieses Buch vorstellt, zeigen, wie neuer Raum gestaltet werden kann und wie Räume, die einst anderen, sehr unterschiedlichen Zwecken dienten (Industrie, Steinbruch, Ladeplatz für Schiffe und sogar ein ehemaliges Gefängnis), umgestaltet werden können.

Die Gartengestaltung, die nicht Gegenstand dieser Zusammenstellung ist, wird nur als ein Element in einigen Innenhöfen von Institutionen, Unternehmen und Parks gezeigt. Die meisten der vorgestellten Plätze sind mittelgroß und liegen weit vom Stadtkern entfernt. Manchmal handelt es sich auch um Entwürfe, die mit der Stadtplanung in den Vorstädten einhergehen.

La arquitectura del paisaje, cuya denominación ha sido acuñada por Gilbert Laing Meason en su obra *Landscape Architecture of the Great Painters of Italy* (Londres, 1828), es una disciplina que aúna diseño, planificación, gestión, preservación y rehabilitación de la tierra. Dicha modalidad permite al profesional paisajista –cuya tarea a veces es «ocupada» por los propios arquitectos– moldear el terreno y modelar el espacio en torno a una pieza arquitectónica ya existente o un plan urbanístico o regional en desarrollo.

De resultas de todo ello, el arquitecto paisajista, tal como un pintor o escultor, logra ser a menudo el transcriptor más poético del lenguaje asociado a cualquier cálculo arquitectónico. El soporte físico animado (planta, árbol, agua, clima) e inanimado (pavimento, superficie, mobiliario) con el que trabaja dicho profesional parte de un contexto geográfico y social (urbano, periurbano y rural) y unos condicionantes técnicos y económicos; su imaginación aporta el resto para dar con una respuesta creativa, competente y lúdica.

Los objetivos del paisajismo se encuentran a menudo a merced de un desarrollo urbanístico ya establecido. En determinadas circunstancias su vocación última reside en la protección medioambiental o del patrimonio histórico, o resulta ser un mero alegato artístico para ciudades exhibicionistas con disposición y recursos para ello. En todas sus acepciones, sin embargo, el diseño de espacios públicos debería responder a su fin principal: la satisfacción de la demanda para su uso social, contemplativo y recreativo.

El medio centenar de proyectos aquí presentes muestran principalmente el diseño de espacios nuevos y la exitosa recuperación de otros con usos anteriores bien diversos (centro industrial, cantera, cargadero naval e incluso un centro penitenciario).

El diseño de jardines, que no era el objeto de esta colección, sólo se presenta de forma más o menos evidente como elemento de algunos patios interiores de condominios, empresas y parques; el grueso de la selección discurre mayoritariamente por espacios de escala mediana y distantes del núcleo urbano, o como elementos consustanciales de un desarrollo urbanístico periurbano.

Le paysagisme, abordé pour la première fois par Gilbert Laing Meason, dans son œuvre *Landscape Architecture of the Great Painters of Italy* (Londres, 1828), est une discipline réunissant design, planification, gestion, préservation et réhabilitation de la terre. Ces modalités permettent au paysagiste professionnel –dont les tâches sont parfois « monopolisées » par les architectes eux-mêmes– de façonner le terrain et modeler l'espace autour d'une œuvre architecturale déjà existante ou un plan d'urbanisation régional en cours de développement.

En fin de compte, l'architecte paysagiste, à l'instar d'un peintre ou d'un sculpteur, devient souvent le transcripteur plus poétique du langage associé à tout calcul d'architecture. Le support physique animé (plante, arbre, eau, climat) et inanimé (carrelage, superficie, mobilier) outils du professionnel en question, fait partie d'un contexte géographique et social (urbain, périurbain et rural) et dépend de conditions techniques et économiques. L'imagination du paysagiste fait le reste pour donner une réponse créative, compétente et ludique.

Les objectifs du paysagisme sont souvent à la merci d'un développement urbanistique pré-établi. Dans certaines conditions, son rôle ultime est de protéger le milieu ambiant ou le patrimoine historique, ou n'être qu'une simple allégation artistique dans des villes pilotes dotées d'un contexte et de moyens pour le faire. Néanmoins, dans tous ces cas de figures, le design d'espaces publiques doit répondre à son objectif principal : satisfaire la demande pour son usage social, contemplatif et récréatif.

La cinquantaine de projets présentés dans cet ouvrage montre surtout le design de nouveaux espaces et la parfaite réhabilitation de lieux aux usages antérieurs très divers (centre industriel, carrière, cargue navale y compris un centre pénitencier).

Le design de jardin, qui n'est pas l'objectif de cette collection, n'apparaît que sous forme plus ou moins évidente, à l'instar d'éléments de quelques patios intérieurs de condominiums, entreprises et parcs : l'essentiel de la sélection évolue surtout autour d'espaces d'échelle moyenne, éloignés du noyau urbain, ou d'éléments inhérents au développement urbain ou périurbain.

Il termine architettura del paesaggio, è stato coniato da Gilbert Laing Meason nella sua opera *Landscape Architecture of the Great Painters of Italy* (Londra, 1828). La disciplina a cui il termine si riferisce riunisce in sé il disegno, la pianificazione, la gestione, la preservazione e la riabilitazione del territorio. Ciò permette al paesaggista – il cui campo di lavoro è a volte invaso dagli architetti – di modellare il terreno e lo spazio che circondano un'opera architettonica già esistente o di agire su un piano di sviluppo urbanistico o regionale.

Spesso, così, l'architetto paesaggista, come un pittore o uno scultore, riesce a trascrivere nel modo più poetico il linguaggio associato a qualsiasi calcolo architettonico. Il supporto fisico con cui lavora – sia esso dinamico (pianta, albero, acqua, condizioni atmosferiche) o statico (pavimentazione, superficie, arredo urbano) – è legato a un contesto geografico e sociale (urbano, periurbano e rurale) e a dei vincoli tecnici ed economici. Il resto è affidato alla sua immaginazione per trovare una soluzione creativa, competente e ludica.

Gli obiettivi del paesaggismo sono spesso alla mercè di un piano urbanistico prestabilito che, se in alcune circostanze è volto a salvaguardare l'ambiente o il patrimonio storico, in altre è un semplice vezzo artistico per città esibizioniste che dispongono della volontà e delle risorse adeguate. Ad ogni modo, ogni piano dovrebbe comunque soddisfare un requisito fondamentale: quello di garantire un uso sociale, riflessivo e ricreativo dello spazio pubblico.

Il mezzo centinaio di progetti che qui si presentano illustrano prevalentemente il disegno di nuovi spazi o la riuscita riabilitazione di altri con un uso anteriore ben distinto (area industriale, miniera, piattaforma di carico per le navi e perfino un centro penitenziario).

Il disegno di giardini, che non è oggetto di questa collezione, è stato trattato in maniera più o meno approfondita solo come elemento associato a alcuni cortili interni di condomini o di aziende e ai parchi.

I progetti presentati sono stati realizzati, per la maggior parte, in spazi di dimensioni medie distanti dai centri abitati, oppure fanno parte di uno sviluppo urbanistico periurbano.

100 LANDSCHAFTSARCHITEKTUR/THILO FOLKERTS | BERLIN, GERMANY
SPAX | BIEL, SWITZERLAND

Websites	www.100land.de | www.tfolkerts.de | www.spax.cc
Project	Escalier d'Eau
Location	Sevélin, Lausanne, Switzerland
Year of completion	2004
Materials	gravel, water
Photo credits	Sébastien Secchi

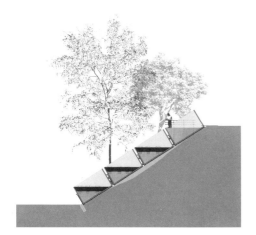

In the Pont Chauderon area in the Flon valley within Laussane's urban center, you can find lands of diverse usage which house industrial equipment and storage areas. Taking the manufacturing context as reference, the landscape architects decided to combine the characteristics of the place –a sloped terrain with a subterranean channel– with the proximity of the park where they store containers, in order to create an "industrialized" park. Conceived as a temporary six-month project, they projected a stairway formed by joining four containers. Of these, the first was filled with gravel, while the rest contained water, gravel and water lilies. Currently, in this space one can find a conventional stairway.

In der Zone an der Brücke Pont Chauderon im Flon-Tal und Stadtzentrum von Lausane befinden sich unterschiedlich genutzte Gelände mit Industrielagern und Geräten. Dieser industrielle Kontext wurde als Referenz genommen. Deshalb kombinierten die Landschaftsplaner die Charakteristika des Orts, ein geneigtes Gelände mit einem unterirdischen Kanal, mit dem nahegelegenen Park, in dem Container gelagert sind. So entstand ein „industrialisierter" Garten. Die für einen Zeitraum von sechs Monaten geschaffene Anlage wurde treppenförmig durch das Aneinanderreihen von vier Containern angelegt. Der obere ist mit Kieselsteinen aufgefüllt, während sich in den anderen Wasser, Kieselsteine und Seerosen befinden. In der Gegenwart befindet sich dort eine normale Treppe.

En la zona de Pont Chauderon, en el valle de Flon y dentro del núcleo urbano de Laussane, se encuentran unos terrenos de uso mixto, que albergan equipamientos y zonas de almacenaje industrial. Tomando como referencia el contexto fabril, los paisajistas decidieron combinar las características del sitio –un terreno en pendiente, secundado por un canal subterráneo– con la proximidad de un parque donde se almacenan contenedores, para crear así un jardín «industrializado». Ideado como un proyecto temporal de seis meses, se proyectó una escalera formada por la sucesión de cuatro contenedores. De éstos, el superior estaba relleno de grava, mientras que el resto contenía agua, grava y nenúfares. Actualmente el espacio está ocupado por una escalera convencional.

La zone du Pont Chauderon, située dans la vallée de Flon et à l'intérieur du centre urbain de Lausanne, dispose de terrains à usage mixte qui abritent des équipements et des zones d'entrepôt industriel. Prenant le contexte manufacturier pour référence, les paysagistes ont décidé de combiner les caractéristiques du site –un terrain en pente, doté d'un canal souterrain– à proximité d'un parc où l'on entrepose des containers, pour créer un jardin « industrialisé ». Pour ce projet temporaire d'une durée de six mois, ils ont conçu un escalier formé de quatre containers successifs. Parmi les quatre, celui du dessus était rempli de graviers, alors que les autres contenaient de l'eau, des graviers et des nénuphars. A l'heure actuelle, l'espace est occupé par un escalier conventionnel.

Nella zona di Pont Chauderon, nella valle di Flon e all'interno del nucleo urbano di Losanna, ci sono alcuni terreni a uso misto in cui si trovano attrezzature e magazzini industriali. Tenendo conto del contesto della zona, gli architetti del paesaggio hanno deciso di combinare le caratteristiche del sito – un terreno in discesa attraversato da un canale sotterraneo – e un vicino parco – usato come deposito di container – per creare un giardino industriale. Il progetto è temporaneo, concepito per una durata di sei mesi, e consiste in una scala formata da quattro container disposti in successione. Di questi, il primo è stato riempito di ghiaia, mentre gli altri con acqua, ghiaia e ninfee. Attualmente il progetto è stato sostituito da una scala tradizionale.

ADHOC MSL/JUAN ANTONIO SÁNCHEZ,
CARLOS JURADO, CARIDAD DE LA PEÑA | MURCIA, SPAIN

Website	www.adhocmsl.com
Project	Alto de Bayna Lookout
Location	Blanca, Spain
Year of completion	2004
Materials	steel
Photo credits	David Frutos Ruiz

"You drive down that road that runs into a narrow valley half way down into one of its hillsides. Suddenly your gaze fixes on a bridge that crosses the river that accompanies you. You stop, get out of the vehicle and approach the bridge. You start walking on it and you stop when you get to the center, then you watch the water running under your feet and dream for a little while. After an indefinite period of time passes, you turn around and get back on your way." The memory of a landscape devoid of highways inspired the design of this raised walkway. Fruit of the idea of levitating, of floating over the landscape, Adhoc projected a structure of sheets of iron painted gold, which go well with the color of its surroundings. At night, the fiber optics at the end of the brace serves as reference against the void.

„**Du fährst über diese** Landstraße, die auf halber Höhe der Hänge durch ein enges Tal führt. Plötzlich trifft dein Blick auf eine Brücke, die den Fluss überquert, an dem du entlang fährst. Du hältst an, steigst aus deinem Auto und näherst dich der Brücke. Du gehst zu Fuß über die Brücke, und wenn du in der Mitte bist, hältst du an, um das Wasser unter deinen Füßen zu betrachten und ein wenig zu träumen. Irgendwann gehst du zurück und setzt deine Reise fort." Die Erinnerung an eine Landschaft ohne Hindernisse inspirierte die Planer zu dieser schwebenden Fußgängerbrücke. Adhoc hat die Struktur aus goldfarben gestrichenen Eisenplatten, deren Farbe sich an die Umgebung anpasst, so entworfen, dass man das Gefühl hat, über der Landschaft zu schweben. Nachts warnt die Glasfaser am Ende des Trägers vor dem Abgrund.

«**Conduces por esa carretera** que recorre un estrecho valle a media altura de una de sus laderas. De súbito tu mirada se detiene en un puente que cruza el río que acompañas. Te detienes, bajas del vehículo y te acercas al puente. Avanzas a pie sobre él y cuando llegas al centro te paras, te dedicas entonces a ver el agua correr bajo tus pies y sueñas un poco. Pasado un tiempo indefinido, regresas y sigues tu camino.» El recuerdo de la visión del paisaje libre de cortapisas inspira el diseño de esta pasarela en voladizo. Fruto de la idea de levitar, de flotar sobre el paisaje, Adhoc ha proyectado una estructura de planchas de hierro pintadas de color dorado, que se adaptan cromáticamente al entorno. Por las noches, la fibra óptica en la parte final del tirante nos sirve de referencia ante el vacío.

« **Tu conduis sur cette route** qui file le long d'une vallée étroite à mi hauteur d'un de ses versants. Subitement, ton regard s'arrête sur un pont qui traverse le fleuve que tu longes. Tu t'arrêtes, descends du véhicule et t'approches du pont. Tu avances à pied et arrivé au centre, tu t'arrêtes. Alors tu te mets à regarder l'eau qui court sous tes pieds et à rêver un instant. Après un temps indéfini, tu rentres et poursuis ton chemin ». Le souvenir ce paysage libre de toute entrave inspire le design de cette passerelle en saillie. Partant de l'idée de léviter, de flotter au-dessus du paysage, Adhoc a conçu une structure en planches de fer peintes en doré, qui s'adaptent chromatiquement à l'environnement. La nuit, la fibre optique, au bout du tirant, nous sert de référence face au vide.

«**Guidi su quella strada** che corre a mezza altezza lungo uno dei versanti di una stretta valle. All'improvviso il tuo sguardo si arresta su un ponte che attraversa il fiume che stai seguendo. Ti fermi, scendi dalla macchina e ti avvicini al ponte. Avanzi a piedi sopra di esso e quando arrivi alla metà ti fermi, guardi l'acqua scorrere sotto i tuoi piedi e sogni, un po'. Dopo un tempo imprecisato, torni indietro e prosegui per la tua strada». Il ricordo dello spettacolo di un paesaggio privo di ostacoli suggerisce il disegno di questa passerella in aggetto. Ispirandosi all'idea di levitare, di galleggiare sul paesaggio, Adhoc ha progettato una struttura di lamine di ferro dipinte in color oro, che si adattano cromaticamente all'ambiente circostante. Di notte, la fibra ottica posta sulla parte finale del tirante è l'ultimo punto di riferimento prima del vuoto.

AP ATELIER/JOSEF PLESKOT | PRAGUE, CZECH REPUBLIC

Website   www.arch.cz/pleskot
Project   Pedestrian Walkway of Deer Moat
Location   Prague, Czech Republic (Prague)
Year of completion 2002
Materials   brick, stone, steel, concrete
Photo credits   Jan Malý

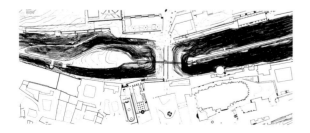

An initiative of the Czech Republic's president, this project joins the Prague Castle with the Vltava River. This subterranean passage, which crosses under a forest area of pronounced slope, makes it easier to get to the castle from the city center since, up until now, visitors had to follow the torturous uphill paths of the city's historical center. The new access follows the course of a stream which descends from the mountain to the Vltava River. In the central area one finds a 255 ft. oval tunnel lined with bricks. Its pavement surface is composed of concrete in one part and steel in another as it crosses just above the running stream. The expressive concrete walls you find when entering and exiting the tunnel contrast with the stone paving and small acequias that hold water.

A l'initiative du président de la république Tchèque, le projet relie le fleuve Vltava au château de Prague. Ce passage souterrain, qui traverse une zone boisée très pentue, facilite énormément l'accès au château depuis le centre urbain. En effet, avant, le visiteur devait emprunter les chemins tortueux en pente de la vieille ville. Le nouvel accès suit le cours d'un canal qui descend de la montagne vers le fleuve Vltava. Dans la zone centrale du passage, on trouve un tunnel ovale de 78 m, revêtu de briques. Le revêtement est fragmenté de bandes de béton et d'autres en acier, juste au-dessus de l'écoulement des eaux. Les murs expressifs en béton de la zone d'entrée et de sortie du tunnel contrastent sur le plan formel avec le revêtement de dalles de pierres et les petits canaux d'irrigation où l'eau s'accumule.

Auf Initiative des Präsidenten der Tschechischen Republik entstand eine Konstruktion, durch die der Fluss Vltava mit der Prager Burg verbunden wird. Mit dieser Passage, die einen sehr steilen Wald unterirdisch durchquert, wird der Zugang zur Burg im Stadtzentrum stark vereinfacht. Bisher mussten die Besucher durch die steilen Gassen, die sich durch die Altstadt schlängeln, zur Burg hochsteigen. Der neue Zugang folgt dem Kanal, der vom Berg zum Fluss Vltava hinunterführt. Im mittleren Bereich der Passage liegt ein 78 m langer, ovaler Tunnel, der mit Ziegelstein verkleidet ist. Der Bodenbelag unterteilt sich in eine Strecke aus Beton und eine aus Stahl, genau über dem Wasser. Die ausdrucksvollen Betonmauern am Ein- und Ausgang des Tunnels bilden einen starken Kontrast zu dem Bodenbelag aus Stein und den kleinen Pflastersteinen in dem Bereich, in dem das Wasser gestaut ist.

Frutto dell'iniziativa del presidente della Repubblica Ceca, questo progetto collega il fiume Vltava con il castello di Praga. Il nuovo passaggio sotterraneo, che attraversa un pendio boscoso di notevole pendenza, facilita considerevolmente l'accesso al castello dal centro urbano visto che, fino ad ora, i visitatori erano costretti a seguire i vicoli ripidi e tortuosi del centro storico della città. Il nuovo accesso corre parallelo al corso di un canale che, dalla collina, scende verso il fiume Vltava. La zona centrale del passaggio è composta da un tunnel ovale lungo 78 m rivestito in mattoni. Il pavimento si divide in una striscia in cemento e in un'altra in acciaio proprio sopra il punto in cui circola l'acqua. Gli espressivi muri in cemento delle zone di entrata e di uscita del tunnel contrastano formalmente con la pavimentazione in pietra e i piccoli canali dove ristagna l'acqua.

Por iniciativa del presidente de la república Checa, el proyecto conecta el río Vltava con el Castillo de Praga. Con dicho pasaje, que atraviesa de forma subterránea una zona boscosa de pendiente pronunciada, se facilita sobremanera el acceso al castillo desde el centro urbano, ya que, hasta la fecha, el visitante debía seguir los caminos tortuosos y en subida que dibuja el casco antiguo de la ciudad. El nuevo acceso sigue el cauce de un canal que desciende desde el monte hasta el río Vltava. En la zona central del pasaje se encuentra un túnel ovalado de 78 m y revestido de ladrillo. Su pavimento se fragmenta en un vial de hormigón y otro de acero, justo sobre el circular de las aguas. Los expresivos muros de hormigón de la zona de entrada y salida del túnel contrastan formalmente con el pavimento de losas de piedra y las pequeñas acequias donde se estanca el agua.

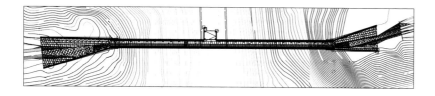

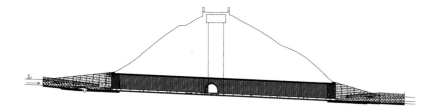

ARRIOLA & FIOL ARQUITECTES / ANDREU ARRIOLA & CARME FIOL | BARCELONA, SPAIN

Website	www.arriolafiol.com
Project	Gran Via de Llevant
Location	Barcelona, Spain
Year of completion	2004
Materials	concrete, corten steel, asphalt finish
Photo credits	Arriola & Fiol arquitectes

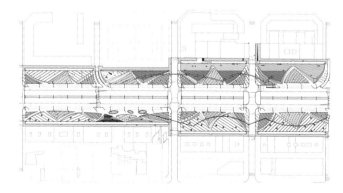

The Gran Via (1.5 miles long by 328 feet wide) forms part of Barcelona's urban periphery landscape. It first appeared in Ildefonso Cerdà's Project of 1867, where it was originally a path surrounded by poplars which, due to the massive immigration during the 60's, ended up becoming a noisy highway. The reconstruction seeks to perfect the landscape as well as improve the acoustics and infrastructure. Arriola & Fiol set out with the purpose of creating a "green valley" that delimits a subterranean road surrounded by acoustic screens. In this valley they've planted poplars, renovated the existing street furniture and built bridges for cars and pedestrians about every 330 feet.

Die Gran Via (2,5 km lang und 100 m breit) bildet einen wichtigen Teil der Stadtlandschaft Barcelonas. Sie entstand nach einem städtebaulichen Entwurf von Ildefonso Cerdà aus dem Jahr 1876. Ursprünglich handelte es sich um eine von Pappeln gesäumte Straße, die aufgrund der massiven Einwanderung in die Stadt in den Sechzigerjahren zu einer lauten Hauptverkehrsader wurde. Durch die Umgestaltung sollte sie landschaftlich schöner gestaltet, die Infrastruktur verbessert und der Lärm vermindert werden. Arriola & Fiol gingen von der Grundidee aus, ein „grünes Tal" zu schaffen, das die unterirdische Straße, die von Schallschutzschirmen umgeben ist, begrenzt. In diesem Tal wurden Pappeln gepflanzt, das existierende städtische Mobiliar erneuert, und ungefähr alle hundert Meter erheben sich schwebende Brücken für Fahrzeuge und Fußgänger.

La Gran Via (2,5 km de largo por 100 m de ancho) forma parte del paisaje periurbano de Barcelona. Surgida del Plan Ildefonso Cerdà de 1876, originariamente era una vía rodeada de chopos que, debido a la masiva inmigración de los años sesenta del siglo pasado, acabó convertida en una ruidosa autopista. La renovación persigue un perfeccionamiento paisajístico, así como una mejora infraestructural y acústica. Arriola & Fiol parten con el propósito de crear un «valle verde» que delimite la carretera subterránea cercada con pantallas acústicas. En dicho valle han plantado chopos, han renovado el mobiliario existente y, cada 100 m aproximadamente, han elevado pasarelas voladizas para coches y viandantes.

La Gran Via (2,5 km long et 100 m de large) fait partie du paysage périurbain de Barcelone. Née du « Plan Ildefonso Cerdà » de 1876, c'était à l'origine une route entourée de peupliers. Dû à l'immigration massive des années soixante du siècle passé, elle a fini par se transformer en autoroute bruyante. La rénovation envisage un perfectionnement du paysage, l'amélioration infrastructurelle et acoustique. Le cabinet Arriola & Fiol part de l'idée de créer un « vallée verte » qui délimite la route souterraine entourée d'écrans phoniques. La vallée en question est plantée de peupliers, équipée d'un mobilier rénové, et, tous les 100 m environ, de passerelles suspendues pour les voitures et les promeneurs.

La Gran Vía (lunga 2,5 km e larga 100 m) fa parte del paesaggio periurbano di Barcellona. Frutto del piano Ildefonso Cerdà del 1876, era in origine una strada circondata da pioppi che, a causa dell'imponente immigrazione avvenuta durante gli anni '60 del secolo scorso, si è trasformata in una rumorosa autostrada. Il progetto di rinnovo punta a un perfezionamento paesaggistico e a un miglioramento infrastrutturale e acustico. Il proposito di Arriola & Fiol è stato quello di creare una «valle verde» che racchiuda la strada sotterranea delimitata da pannelli fonoassorbenti. A tale scopo sono stati piantati dei pioppi, sono stati rinnovati gli arredi urbani e, ogni 100 m circa, sono state disposte passerelle sopraelevate per auto e passanti.

ASPECT STUDIOS | SURRY HILLS, AUSTRALIA

Website	www.aspect.net.au
Project	Parramatta Police Headquarters
Location	Parramatta, Australia
Year of completion	2003
Materials	pavement, concrete, timber
Photo credits	Simon Wood

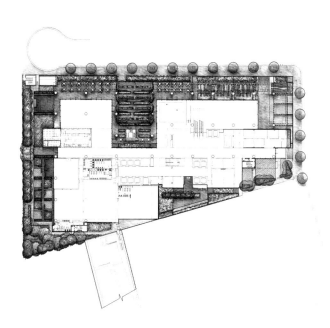

The rest area of the Parramatta Police Department in a suburb west of Sydney is divided into four areas: the entrance patio, the central patio, the West wing and the South wing. Each part was designed differently according to its orientation and the image they wanted to give it; they used pavement and gravel flower beds depending on each space's specific purpose. The paved surfaces were intended to be used for workers to circulate, while the gravel areas are intended for rest areas. Of the four areas, the central patio is the most emblematic since it serves as a nexus between the two wings and also connects the canteens.

Die Ruhezonen der Polizeizentrale in Parramatta, einer Vorstadt im Westen von Sydney, unterteilt sich in vier Bereiche: den Eingangshof, den zentralen Hof, den West- und den Südflügel. Jeder Bereich wurde entsprechend der Lage und dem Bild, das entstehen sollte, anders gestaltet. Je nach Nutzung wählte man als Bodenbelag Pflaster oder Schotter. Die gepflasterten Zonen dienen als Durchgangsbereiche für die Angestellten, während die mit Schotter belegten Bereiche Ruhezonen sind. Die auffallendste Zone ist der zentrale Hof, der auch als Verbindung zwischen den beiden Gebäudeflügeln dient und die Kantinen einbindet.

Las zonas de descanso de la central de Policía de Parramatta, en un suburbio al oeste de Sydney, están divididas en cuatro zonas: el patio de entrada, el patio central, el ala oeste y el ala sur. Cada parte fue diseñada de forma distinta en función de la orientación e imagen a ofrecer; según el uso específico de cada espacio se utilizó pavimento y parterres de grava. Las superficies pavimentadas fueron ideadas como zona de circulación de los trabajadores, mientras que las bandas de grava se relacionan con las áreas de descanso. De las cuatro zonas, el patio central es el espacio más emblemático, ya que sirve de nexo entre las dos alas del edifico y además conecta los comedores.

Les zones de repos du commissariat central de police de Parramatta, dans une banlieue à l'ouest de Sydney, sont divisées en quatre : le patio d'entrée, le patio central, l'aile ouest et l'aile sud. Chaque espace affiche une conception différente en fonction de l'orientation et de l'image à offrir : leur usage spécifique est marqué par du carrelage ou des parterres de gravier. Les superficies carrelées sont conçues comme zone de circulation des travailleurs, alors que les bandes de gravier sont reliées aux aires de repos. Sur les quatre zones, le patio central est l'espace le plus emblématique, car il sert de liaison entre les deux ailes de l'édifice et relie également les restaurants.

L'area di riposo della centrale di polizia di Parramatta, situata in una zona residenziale a ovest di Sydney, è suddivisa in quattro parti: il cortile d'ingresso, il cortile centrale, l'ala ovest e l'ala sud. Ognuna di queste parti è stata progettata in modo diverso in funzione dell'orientazione e dell'immagine che si è voluto proporre. A seconda dell'uso a cui è adibito ogni spazio si è scelto il selciato o il parterre di ghiaia. Le superfici selciate sono state concepite come zone di circolazione, mentre le aree di ghiaia sono adibite al relax. Delle quattro zone, il cortile centrale è lo spazio più significativo, in quanto funziona da nesso tra le due ali dell'edificio e collega le mense dei lavoratori.

BALMORI ASSOCIATES | NEW YORK, USA

Website	www.balmori.com
Project	Campa de los Ingleses
Location	Bilbao, Spain
Renderings	Balmori Associates

With the aim of subjugating urban landscape, architecture and public space in a single project, Balmori Associates won the competition that forms part of the master plan for Abandoibarra, projected in 1997 together with Pelli Clarke Pelli and Aguinaga & Associates. As a result of this plan they will completely regenerate the space between the Guggenheim Bilbao Musuem and the Euskalduna Jauregia Bilbao Conference and Music Center. The design proposed by the New York studio combines curved terraces –with a mountainous landscape with a maximum drop of 33 ft.–, elliptical silhouettes and pedestrian overpasses. The project emphasizes for relaxing and looking at the Nervion River, the mountain and the Guggenheim.

Balmori Associates gewann diese Ausschreibung, deren Ziel es war, die Stadtlandschaft, die Architektur und den öffentlichen Raum miteinander in Einklang zu bringen. Die Ausschreibung bildet einen Teil des Bebauungsplans für Abandoibarra, erstellt 1997 zusammen mit Pelli Clarke Pelli und Aguinaga & Associates. Aufgrund dieses Plans wird der städtische Raum zwischen dem Guggenheim-Museum in Bilbao und dem Kongress- und Musikpalast Euskalduna vollständig umgestaltet. Der Gestaltungsvorschlag des Studios in New York kombiniert gebogene Terrassen, die eine Landschaft mit Höhenunterschieden von bis zu 10 m bilden, mit Ellipsenformen und Fußgängerwegen. Besondere Bedeutung wurde den Zonen zugemessen, in denen man sich entspannen und auf den Fluss Nervión, das umliegende Gebirge oder das Guggenheim schauen kann.

Con el objetivo de subyugar paisaje urbano, arquitectura y espacio público en una misma propuesta, Balmori Associates ganó esta competición que forma parte del master plan para Abandoibarra, proyectado en 1997 junto con Pelli Clarke Pelli y Aguinaga & Associates. Como fruto de dicho plan se regenerará totalmente el espacio ubicado entre el Museo Guggenheim Bilbao y el Palacio Euskalduna de Congresos y de la Música. El diseño propuesto por el estudio neoyorquino combina las terrazas curvadas –a modo de un paisaje en relieve con un desnivel máximo de 10 m–, las siluetas elípticas y los pasos peatonales. El proyecto hace hincapié en los espacios para relajarse y mirar el río Nervión, la montaña o el Guggenheim.

Avec comme objectif de soumettre paysage urbain, architecture et espace public dans une même proposition, Balmori Associates ont remporté ce concours qui fait partie du plan d'ensemble master plan pour Abandoibarra, projeté en 1997 avec Pelli Clarke Pelli et Aguinaga & Associates. Le plan en question concerne la réhabilitation complète de l'espace situé entre le Musée Guggenheim Bilbao et le Palais Euskalduna des Congrès et de la Musique. Le design proposé par le cabinet d'études new-yorkais conjugue terrasses incurvées –à l'instar d'un paysage en relief avec une dénivellation maximale de 10 m–, silhouettes elliptiques et zones piétonnes. Le projet met l'accent sur les espaces pour se détendre en regardant la rivière Nervión, la montagne ou le Guggenheim.

Fondendo paesaggio urbano, architettura e spazio pubblico, la proposta dello studio Balmori Associates, in collaborazione con Pelli Clarke Pelli y Aguinaga & Associates, ha vinto nel 1997 il concorso per il master plan di Abandoibarra. Il progetto prevede una riconfigurazione integrale dello spazio compreso tra il Museo Guggenheim e il Palazzo Euskalduna dei Congressi e della Musica, combinando terrazze curve – che creano una specie di paesaggio in rilievo con un dislivello massimo di 10 m –, profili ellittici e passaggi pedonali. L'obiettivo è quello di creare spazi per il relax, dai quali sia possibile ammirare il fiume Nervión, le montagne e il Guggenheim.

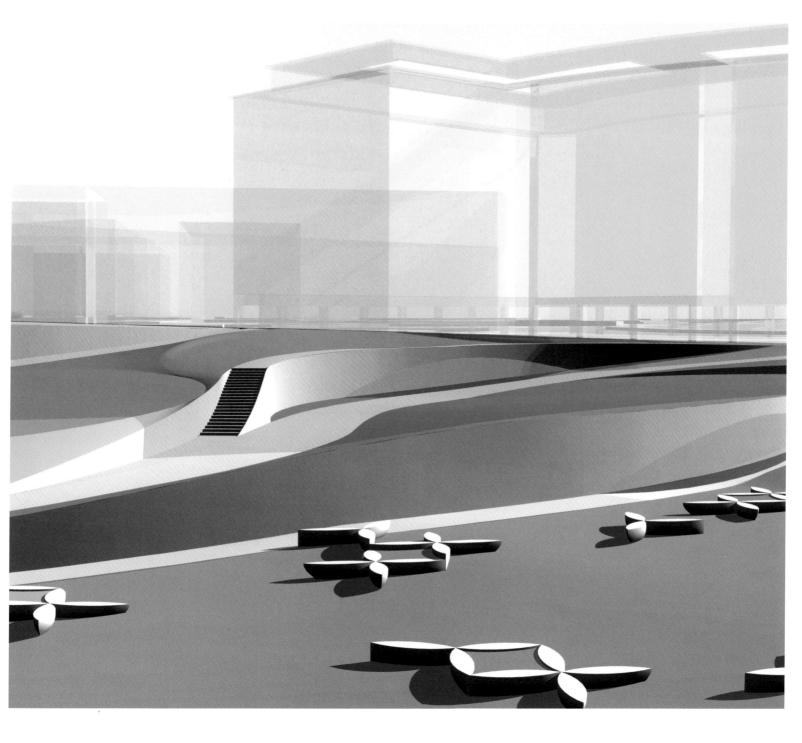

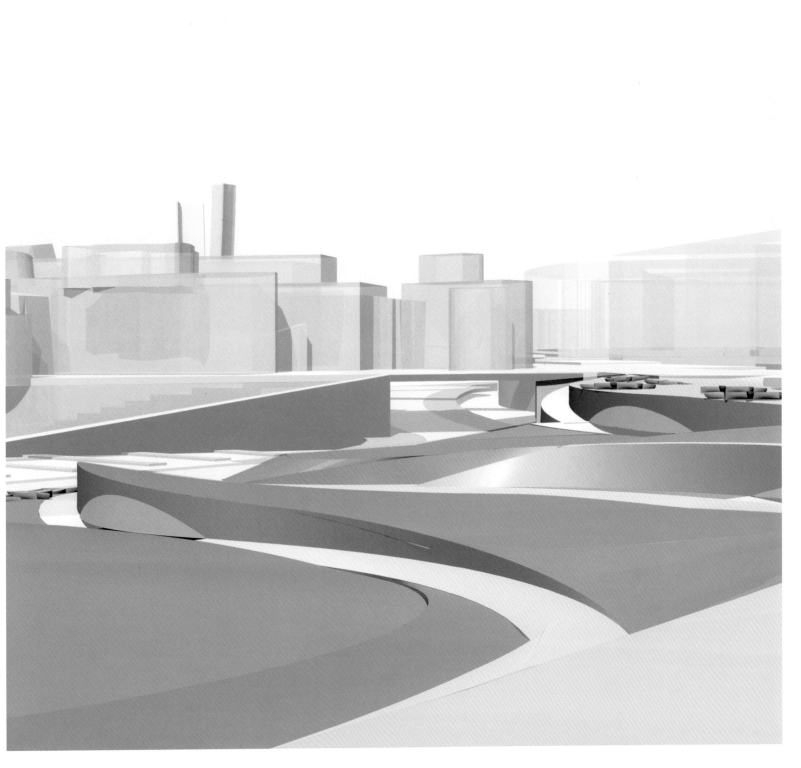

BURGER LANDSCHAFTSARCHITEKTEN | MUNICH, GERMANY

Website	www.burgerlandschaftsarchitekten.de
Project	Green Axis 13
Location	Messestadt Riem, Munich, Germany
Year of completion	2006
Materials	wood, concrete, gravel, macadam
Photo credits	Florian Holzherr

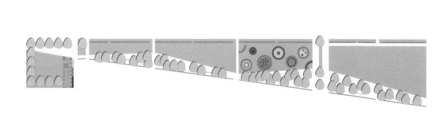

Located in **Messestadt Riem,** a young neighborhood east of Munich that occupies the area of the old Munich-Riem airport (closed in 1992); this park spreads from north to south between residential areas. Green Axis 13 has been projected as a green passage that flows into another park on its south side and serves to connect a developed area with an undeveloped one. The axis is marked by a gravel path joined by rest areas, grass fields and recreational parks (Playground of Transversal Games). On its north end it is complemented with a Pocket Park and on the South-West side with a pavilion that will eventually serve as a meeting point and a place to store equipment.

Dieser Park liegt in der Messestadt Riem, einem neuen Viertel von München, auf dem Gelände des ehemaligen Flughafens München-Riem, der 1992 geschlossen wurde. Er verläuft zwischen Wohngebieten von Norden nach Süden. Die grüne Achse 13 wurde wie ein grüner Korridor angelegt, der auf der Südseite in einen anderen Park mündet und als Verbindung zwischen einer besiedelten Zone und einer unbesiedelten Region dient. Durch den Park verläuft ein von Ruhezonen gesäumter Schotterweg, und es gibt Rasen-, Freizeit- und Spielflächen. An der Nordseite liegt ein Pocket-Park, im Südosten ein Pavillon, der als Treffpunkt und zur Aufbewahrung von Geräten dient.

Situado en Messestadt Riem, un barrio joven al este de Munich y que ocupa los terrenos del antiguo aeropuerto München-Riem (cerrado en 1992), este parque discurre de norte a sur entre zonas residenciales. Green Axis 13 ha sido proyectado como un corredor verde que desemboca en otro parque por el flanco sur y sirve de conexión entre un espacio urbanizado y otro sin urbanizar. El axis viene marcado por un paseo de grava secundado por áreas de reposo, campos de césped y parques recreativos (Playground of Transversal Games). Se complementa, por el flanco norte, con un Pocket Park y, en la parte sur-oeste, con un pabellón que eventualmente sirve como punto de encuentro y donde se guarda el equipamiento.

Situé à Riem, ville de foire, dans un jeune quartier à l'est de Munich qui occupe les terrains de l'ancien aéroport München-Riem (fermé en 1992), ce parc s'étend du nord au sud entre les zones résidentielles. Green Axis 13 est conçu comme un couloir de verdure qui débouche sur un autre parc sur le flanc sud et sert de lien entre un espace urbanisé et un autre sans urbanisation. L'axe est marqué par une promenade en gravier agrémentée d'aires de repos, champs de gazon et parcs récréatifs (Terrain de jeux de Transversal Games). Il est complété au sud par un « Pocket Park » et au sud-ouest, par un pavillon qui peut servir de lieu de rencontre et/ou de stockage de l'équipement.

Questo parco, ubicato nel Messestadt Riem, un quartiere giovane nella parte est di Monaco, occupa il terreno del vecchio aeroporto München-Riem (chiuso nel 1992) e corre in direzione nord-sud attraverso zone residenziali. Il Green Axis 13 è stato progettato come un corridoio verde che sbocca in un altro parco nel suo lato sud e serve da connessione tra uno spazio urbanizzato e uno non urbanizzato. L'asse è marcato da un viale di ghiaia contornato da aree per il relax, prati e parchi giochi (Playground of Transversal Games). Lo completano, nel lato nord, il Pocket Park e, nella parte sudovest, un padiglione che serve da punto d'incontro e è usato per riporre le attrezzature.

BURGER LANDSCHAFTSARCHITEKTEN | MUNICH, GERMANY

Website	www.burgerlandschaftsarchitekten.de
Project	Unterföhring Park Village
Location	Munich, Germany
Year of completion	2003
Materials	wachenzell dolomite
Photo credits	Florian Holzherr
Site plan layout	Rakete

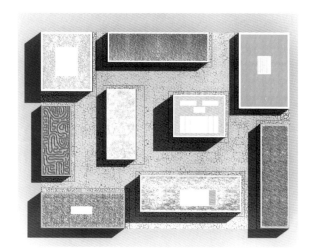

The master plan for this office area consists of a main skeleton formed by a "village" with 19 different rectangular buildings. The first phase was completed by raising nine buildings which gave the set its heterogeneity. The challenge was to complement the diversity in volumes with an urban space that unified the landscape. They developed two levels to accomplish this: a lower level consisting of a plaza with slabs of polygonal stone separated by grass; and a second level where they projected a series of landscaped rooftops with a diverse and colorful design that emphasized the independence of each building with their varying heights.

Der Bebauungsplan für diese Zone mit Bürogebäuden zeichnet eine Art Skelett als Grundstruktur, das aus einer Siedlung mit 19 verschiedenen, rechteckigen Gebäuden besteht. Die erste Phase wurde mit der Errichtung von neun Gebäuden fertiggestellt, die sehr unterschiedlich sind. Es war nun eine Herausforderung an die Landschaftsplaner, diese so verschiedenartigen Gebäude durch eine urbane Grünzone zu ergänzen, die ein einheitliches Bild entstehen lässt. Dazu wurde auf zwei Ebenen gearbeitet. Auf der der unteren Ebene schuf man einen Platz, gepflastert mit vieleckigen Steinplatten, die durch Grasstreifen voneinander getrennt sind. Auf der zweiten Ebene legte man eine Reihe begrünter Dächer mit unterschiedlicher Aufteilung und Farben an, was noch einmal die Unabhängigkeit der eizelnen Gebäude, die auch unterschiedliche Höhen haben, unterstreicht.

El *master plan* ideado para esta zona de oficinas traza un esqueleto principal formado por un «village» con 19 edificios rectangulares diferentes. La primera fase fue completada con el alzado de nueve edificios que respondiesen a la heterogeneidad del conjunto. El reto paisajístico fue complementar dicha diversidad de volúmenes con un espacio urbano que los uniformase. Para ello se trabajó en dos niveles: uno inferior, compuesto por una plaza con losas de piedra poligonales, separadas por bandas de hierba; y un segundo nivel donde se proyectaron una serie de cubiertas ajardinadas con un diseño diverso y colorido, lo que enfatizó la independencia de cada bloque de altura variable.

Le *master plan* conçu pour cette zone de bureaux, trace un ossature principale formée par un « village » de 19 édifices rectangulaires différents. A la première phase s'est ajoutée la construction de neuf édifices qui répondent à l'hétérogénéité de l'ensemble. Le réseau paysager a complété cette diversité de volumes par un espace urbain qui les uniformise. Pour cela, deux niveaux ont été conçus : un niveau inférieur, composé d'une place de dalles de pierres polygonales, séparée par des bandes d'herbe. Le niveau supérieur accueille une série de toitures dotées de jardins au design divers et coloré, accentuant ainsi l'indépendance de chaque bloc à hauteur variable.

Il *master plan* per questa zona di uffici è composta da uno scheletro formato da un «village» di 19 edifici rettangolari ognuno diverso dagli altri. La prima fase del progetto è stata completata con la costruzione di nove edifici, che riflettono l'eterogeneità dell'insieme. La sfida, dal punto di vista dell'architettura del paesaggio, è stata quella di dare omogeneità a uno spazio urbano caratterizzato da una tale diversità di volumi. L'intervento si è concentrato su due livelli: quello inferiore, formato da una piazza con pavimentazione in lastre poligonali di pietra, separate da strisce d'erba; e quello superiore, formato da una serie di coperture con giardini dal disegno particolare e colorato, che contribuisce a mettere in risalto l'unicità di ognuno dei blocchi di diversa altezza.

C-V HØLMEBAKK | OSLO, NORWAY

Project	Sohlbergplassen Viewpoint
Location	Stor-Elvdal, Norway
Year of completion	2006
Materials	concrete, steel
Photo credits	C-V Hølmebakk, Rickard Riesenfeld

The Norwegian painter Harald Sohlbery (1869-1935) lived in the Rondane Mountains for some years in order to sketch his famous painting *Winter Night in the Mountains*. Based on one of the settings that served as inspiration for the painter, Hølmebakk decided to raise a walkway among the dense pines with views of the lake and mountains. The scenic accomplishment of the project lies in fixing the structure without harming the trees or their root system. The original steel structure was discarded in favor of a concrete one because of the risk of snow and ice in the area. The walkway, with its 1 ft. downward slope, represents the architectural response to the painter's view some decades before.

Der norwegische Maler Harald Sohlberg (1869-1935) lebte jahrelang in dem Berggebiet Rondane, um an den Skizzen seines berühmten Gemäldes „Winternacht in Rondane" zu arbeiten. An einem der Orte, der dem Maler als Inspiration diente, hat Hølmebakk eine Fußgängerbrücke inmitten eines dichten Kiefernwaldes mit Blick auf den See und die Berge konstruiert. Es ist als Erfolg der Landschaftsplaner zu verzeichnen, dass diese Struktur keinerlei Schäden an den Bäumen oder an ihrem Wurzelsystem verursacht hat. Zunächst war eine Stahlstruktur geplant, dann entschied man sich jedoch für Beton, da in dieser Region viel Schnee fällt und es oft friert. Die Fußgängerbrücke mit einer Neigung von 0,3 m ist die architektonische Antwort auf das Gemälde, das der Maler Jahrzehnte vorher geschaffen hat.

El pintor noruego Harald Sohlberg (1869-1935) se instaló durante años en la zona de las montañas Rondane para realizar los bocetos de su famoso cuadro *Winter Night in the Mountains*. Basado en una de las localizaciones que sirvieron como fuente de inspiración al pintor, Hølmebakk decide levantar una pasarela entre una densa pineda con vistas al lago y a las montañas. El logro paisajístico de dicho proyecto ha sido asentar la estructura sin daño alguno ni a los árboles ni a su sistema radicular. La estructura original de acero se descartó por una de hormigón, debido al riesgo que representaba la presencia de nieve y hielo en la zona. La pasarela, con una pendiente de 0,3 m hacia abajo, representa la respuesta arquitectónica a la mirada retenida por el pintor décadas antes.

Le peintre norvégien Harald Sohlberg (1869-1935) s'est installé des années durant dans la zone des montagnes Rondane pour réaliser les esquisses de son célèbre cadre *Winter Night in the Mountains*. S'installant dans un des endroits qui servirent de source d'inspiration à l'auteur, Hølmebakk décide d'ériger une passerelle entre une pinède dense, donnant sur le lac et les montagnes. La réussite du paysagisme de ce projet repose sur l'élévation de la structure, qui ne porte atteinte ni aux arbres ni au système radiculaire. Vu le risque représenté par la neige et la glace dans cette zone, la structure originale en acier a été remplacée par une autre en béton. La passerelle, forte d'une pente de 0,3 m vers le bas, est l'interprétation architecturale du regard fixé sur une toile par le peintre, des dizaines d'années plus tôt.

Il pittore norvegese Harald Sohlberg (1869-1935) visse per anni nella zona delle montagne di Rondane, dove realizzò i bozzetti del suo famoso quadro *Winter Night in the Mountains*. Basandosi in uno dei luoghi che furono fonte di ispirazione per il pittore, Hølmebakk ha progettato una passerella che attraversa una densa pineta e offre viste al lago e alle montagne. Il successo paesaggistico del progetto risiede nel fatto che è stato possibile collocare la struttura senza danneggiare gli alberi o le loro radici; si è deciso di ricorrere al cemento, invece che all'acciaio, a causa del rischio che rappresentano la neve e il ghiaccio, comuni nella zona. La passerella, inclinata di 0,3 m verso il basso, è la risposta architettonica a ciò che lo sguardo del pittore contemplava alcuni decenni fa.

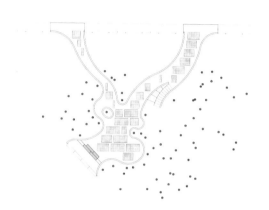

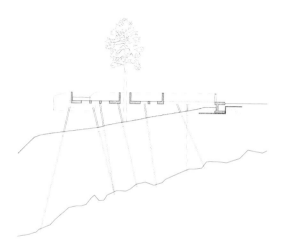

DONALDSON & WARN ARCHITECTS | PERTH, AUSTRALIA

Website	www.donaldsonandwarn.com.au
Project	The Bali Memorial
Location	Perth, Australia
Year of completion	2003
Materials	austen steel, kimberley sandstone, black granite, jarrah and blackbutt timber, glass, bronze, granite boulder, concrete, pavement, limestone
Photo credits	Martin Farquharson

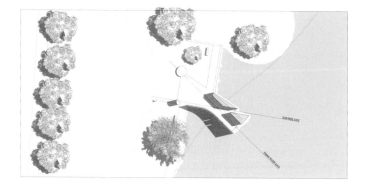

The Bali Memorial aims to be a meeting point and place to reflect on the terrorist attacks of October 12, 2002. The space is formally divided into two axes: one which exalts the view of the Swan River Estuary waters, and another directed towards the line of the horizon where the sun comes up each October 12th. The well-studied distribution of the steel, granite and sandstone walls with which the memorial is built, forms a gateway that filters the morning light, illuminating the attack's commemorative plaque. The project includes collaborations by indigenous writer Sally Morgan and artist Kevin Draper.

Das Bali Memorial ist ein Treffpunkt und ein Ort des Nachdenkens über die terroristischen Attentate vom 12. Oktober 2002. Der Raum unterteilt sich in zwei Achsen; von der einen aus hat man einen wundervollen Blick auf die Mündung des Flusses Swan, und die andere weist auf den Punkt am Horizont, an dem die Sonne jeden 12. Oktober aufgeht. Die geschlossene Gliederung der Mauern aus Stahl, Granit und dem Sandstein des Memorials zeichnet ein Portal, durch das sich das Morgenlicht filtert und das den Platz beleuchtet, der an das Attentat erinnert. An dem Projekt arbeiteten der einheimische Schriftsteller Sally Morgan und der Künstler Kevin Draper mit.

El monumento conmemorativo de Bali pretende ser un polo de encuentro y reflexión en torno a los atentados terroristas del 12 de octubre de 2002. Formalmente el espacio se divide en dos ejes: uno que ensalza la visión de las aguas del estuario del río Swan y otro dirigido al punto del horizonte donde sale el sol cada 12 de octubre. La articulación cerrada de los muros de acero, granito y arenisca con los que se levanta el memorial dibuja un portal por donde se filtra la luz de la mañana, que ilumina la placa de conmemoración del atentado. El proyecto incluye colaboraciones de la escritora indígena Sally Morgan y del artista Kevin Draper.

Le Mémorial de Bali veut être un pôle de rencontre et de réflexion sur les attentats terroristes du 12 octobre 2002. Sur le plan formel, l'espace se divise en deux axes : un qui exalte la vision des eaux de l'estuaire du fleuve Swan et l'autre pointé sur l'horizon d'où le soleil se lève tous les 12 octobre. La distribution fermée des murs en acier, granit et grès qui forment le mémorial, dessine un portail d'où filtre la lumière du jour, illuminant ainsi la plaque de commémoration de l'attentat. L'écrivain indigène Sally Morgan et l'artiste Kevin Draper ont également participé à ce projet.

Il monumento commemorativo di Bali vuole essere un punto d'incontro e una riflessione sugli attentati terroristi del 12 ottobre del 2002. Lo spazio è formalmente suddiviso da due assi: uno che dà rilievo alla vista alle acque dell'estuario del fiume Swan e un altro rivolto verso il punto dell'orizzonte da cui sorge il sole ogni 12 di ottobre. L'articolazione serrata dei muri in acciaio, granito e arenaria che formano il monumento disegna un'entrata attraverso cui penetra la luce del mattino, illuminando la targa che commemora le vittime dell'attentato. Hanno collaborato al progetto la scrittrice aborigena Sally Morgan e l'artista Kevin Draper.

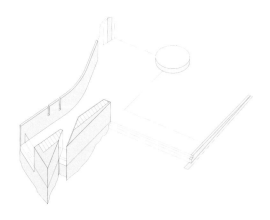

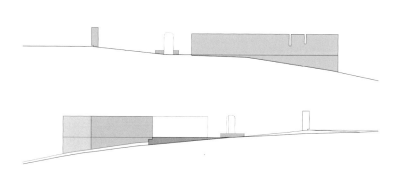

DURBACH BLOCK ARCHITECTS | SYDNEY, AUSTRALIA

Website	www.durbachblock.com
Project	The Brick Pit Ring
Location	Homebush Bay, Sydney, Australia
Year of completion	2005
Materials	concrete, steel, glass
Photo credits	Brett Boardman, Peter Hyatt, Kraig Carlstrom, Roger de Souza, Durbach Block Architects

Presented by the authors themselves as tangible testimony of the vast extraction activity at Homebush Bay, this infrastructure adjusts to the archetypical, primitive and naked shape of a brick-pit that was used for such a long time. Viewed as a metaphor of the indiscriminate exploitation of the land, this thin aerial ring serves as a walkway, as well as an outdoors exhibition area. Built about 65 ft. above the ground, this circular ring forms part of Sydney's Olympic Park and uses two bridges to connect with two parks in the area. The closed nature of the bridges contrasts with the ring's openness.

Die Architekten selbst verstehen ihre Konstruktion mit ihrer urbildlichen, primitiven und nackten Form eines lange ausgebeuteten Steinbruchs als ein greifbares Zeugnis des Steinabbaus in Homebush Bay. Dieser schwebende und schlanke Ring ist eine Metapher für die Ausbeutung der Erde und dient als Durchgangsort und Ausstellungsort im Freien. Die kreisförmige, 20 Meter über dem Boden schwebende Fußgängerbrücke gehört zum Olympiagelände von Sydney und verbindet zwei Parkanlagen in dieser Zone durch zwei Brücken. Die geschlossenen Brücken bilden einen Kontrast zu dem offen gestalteten Ring.

Presentado por sus propios autores como un testimonio tangible de la vasta actividad extractora en Homebush Bay, esta infraestructura responde a la forma arquetípica, primitiva y desnuda de una cantera utilizada durante un largo tiempo. Vista como metáfora de la explotación indiscriminada del terreno, este anillo voladizo y esbelto representa un lugar de tránsito, así como un espacio expositivo al aire libre. Situado a unos 20 m del suelo, esta pasarela circular forma parte del Parque Olímpico de Sydney y conecta, mediante dos puentes, con dos parques de la zona. El carácter cerrado de los puentes contrasta con la planta abierta que dibuja el anillo.

Présenté par ses propres auteurs comme un témoignage tangible de l'importante activité extractrice de Homebush Bay, cette infrastructure répond à la forme archétype, primitive et dénudée d'une carrière exploitée pendant des lustres. Vision métaphorique de l'exploitation indiscriminée du terrain, ce svelte anneau en saillie représente un lieu de transit, ainsi qu'un espace d'exposition en plein air. Suspendue à environ 20 m du sol, cette passerelle circulaire fait partie du Parc Olympique de Sydney et relie, grâce à deux ponts, la structure aux parcs de la zone. Le caractère fermé des ponts contraste avec l'espace ouvert dessiné par l'anneau.

Presentata dagli stessi autori come una prova tangibile della vasta attività di estrazione della baia di Homebush, questa struttura risponde alla forma archetipica, primitiva e spoglia di una miniera sfruttata da lungo tempo. Metafora dello sfruttamento indiscriminato del suolo, questo sottile anello in aggetto è, al tempo stesso, un luogo di transito e uno spazio espositivo all'aria aperta. Sospesa a circa 20 m da terra, questa passerella circolare forma parte del parco olimpico di Sydney e è collegata, attraverso due ponti, a due parchi della zona. L'aspetto chiuso dei ponti fa da contrasto con la pianta aperta dell'anello.

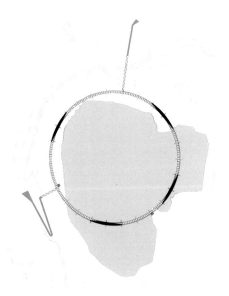

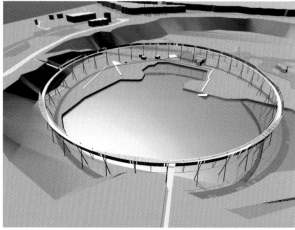

ESTUDIO DEL PAISAJE TERESA MOLLER & ASOCIADOS | SANTIAGO, CHILE

Website	www.teresamoller.cl
Project	Punta Pite
Location	Zapallar, Chile
Year of completion	2005
Materials	stone
Photo credits	Cristobal Palma, Estudio del Paisaje
	Teresa Moller & Asociados

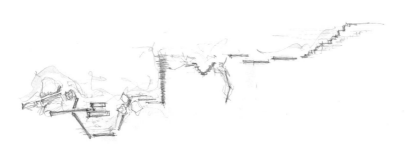

"This project could be considered a revelation of a landscape rather than an intervention, in the sense that various points were set so as to make it possible to go through the area while appreciating it". These are the words of the Chilean studio that was commissioned to intervene in a community with 29 plots for sale, but with geomorphologic characteristics that include complicated access on account of the numerous rocks and small cliffs. The 0.9 mile boulder path joins the territory with the coast and gives a view of a landscape that was previously inaccessible. The intervention, which is of great poetic strength, also incorporates walkways, vantage points of the sea and performances in the Park of the Point thanks to the sculptor Gerardo Aristia.

Dieses Planungsprojekt kann man – statt als einen Eingriff in die Landschaft – als das Auftauchen einer Landschaft bezeichnen, denn es wurden verschiedene Bereiche neugestaltet, von denen aus man den Raum durchschreiten und wirklich genießen kann. So beschreibt ein chilenisches Studio den Auftrag zur landschaftlichen Umgestaltung einer Siedlung, in der 29 Grundstücke zum Verkauf standen. Die Oberflächenform und die Zufahrtsmöglichkeiten zu der Zone stellten aufgrund vieler Felsen und kleiner Steinküsten eine schwierige Herausforderung an die Planer dar. Ein 1,5 km langer, mit Kieselsteinen aufgeschütteter Pfad vereint die Gelände an der Küste und lässt den Blick auf Landschaften frei, die vorher unzugänglich waren. An dieser sehr poetischen Gestaltung voller Laufstege, Ausblickspunkte auf das Meer und Eingriffe in den Park de la Punta wirkte der Bildhauer Gerardo Aristía mit.

«El proyecto se podría considerar como un proyecto de aparición de un paisaje más que de intervención en éste, en el sentido de que fueron habilitados distintos puntos desde los cuales es posible recorrer el lugar al mismo tiempo que apreciarlo.» En estos términos se expresa el estudio chileno que recibió el encargo de intervenir en una comunidad con 29 terrenos a la venta, pero con unas características geomorfológicas de difícil acceso, por las numerosas rocas y los pequeños acantilados. El sendero de piedra canteada de 1,5 km une el territorio por la costa y muestra un paisaje antes inaccesible. La intervención, de alto voltaje poético, también incorpora, con la ayuda del escultor Gerardo Aristía, pasarelas, miradores al mar y actuaciones en el Parque de la Punta.

« Le projet peut être considéré comme un projet de création d'un paysage plus qu'une intervention sur ce dernier. Ceci dans le sens où différents points ont été aménagés d'où l'on peut parcourir le lieu tout en l'appréciant ». C'est ainsi que s'exprime le studio chilien, chargé de l'intervention dans une commune disposant de 29 terrains à la vente, dotés de caractéristiques géomorphologiques d'accès difficile, dû aux nombreux rochers et petites falaises. Le sentier de pierre de carrière de 1,5 km réunit le territoire à la côte, dévoilant ainsi un paysage autrefois inaccessible. L'intervention, hautement poétique, intègre aussi, avec l'aide du sculpteur Gerardo Aristía, passerelles, mirados vers la mer et jeux dans le Parc de la Punta.

«Più che un intervento sul paesaggio questo progetto può essere considerato una rivelazione del paesaggio, nel senso che sono stati creati diversi punti dai quali è possibile percorrere il luogo e, al tempo stesso, apprezzarne la bellezza.» In questi termini si esprime lo studio cileno che ha ricevuto l'incarico di intervenire su un'area con 29 terreni in vendita, ma dall'accesso difficile, a causa delle caratteristiche morfologiche di un terreno in cui abbondano le rocce e i piccoli dirupi. Il sentiero in conci di pietra lungo 1,5 km collega le diverse zone della costa e si apre a un paesaggio prima inaccessibile. Questo progetto ad alto potenziale poetico accoglie inoltre, grazie all'aiuto dello scultore Gerardo Aristía, passerelle, belvedere sul mare e diversi interventi nel Parco della Punta.

FELIPE PEÑA PEREDA, FRANCISCO NOVOA RODRÍGUEZ | LA CORUÑA, SPAIN

Project	Ethnographic Park in Insua
Location	Insua, Lugo, Spain
Year of completion	2002
Materials	granite, laminated wood, stainless steel
Photo credits	Juan Rodríguez

Located in an old iron loading platform in the Ria of Viveiro, the project regenerates the existing landscape with a reconversion that unites its industrial, ethnographical, environmental and recreational legacy. To do this they took advantage of elements of the past —such as the remains of the original steel structure and the 13 ft. high stone walls—, which are combined with an iron structure to form a vantage point on top. The sharp topographical drop, and the way the structure penetrates into the sea, evokes the old loading platform to give greater intrinsic character to a project that manages to give the coastal line some continuity, as well as offering a new place for Sunday strolls and leisure.

Wo einst an der Bucht von Viveiro Eisenmaterial verladen wurde, gestaltete man eine bereits existierende Landschaft so um, dass die industrielle Vergangenheit mit den ethnografischen Aspekten, der Umwelt und der Freizeit verbunden wurde. Dazu benutzte man die Elemente aus der Vergangenheit, z. B. die Überreste der originalen Stahlstruktur und die 4 m hohen Steinmauern, und ergänzte sie mit einer oberen Eisenstruktur, die gleichzeitig als Aussichtsterrasse dient. Die großen Höhenunterschiede und das Eindringen des Meers in die Struktur, das an den alten Ladeplatz erinnert, verleihen dem Ort einen sehr eigenen Charakter. Die Küstenlinie ist nun wieder ununterbrochen nutzbar, und es entstand ein neuer Ort, an dem die Menschen lange Spaziergänge unternehmen und ihre Freizeit verbringen können.

Situado en un antiguo cargadero de mineral de hierro en la ría de Viveiro, el proyecto regenera el paisaje existente con una reconversión que aúna legado industrial, etnografía, medio ambiente y recreación. Para ello aprovecha elementos del pasado —como los restos de la estructura de acero original y los muros de piedra de 4 m de altura— que, complementados con una estructura superior de hierro, se alzan a modo de mirador. El fuerte desnivel topográfico y la penetración en el mar de la estructura que evoca al antiguo cargadero dan aún mayor carácter intrínseco a un proyecto que consigue dar continuidad de uso a la línea de costa, así como ofrece un nuevo lugar para el paseo y ocio dominical.

Situé dans une ancienne cargue de minerai de fer de la vallée fluviale de Viveiro, le projet régénère le paysage existant dans une réhabilitation qui allie héritage industriel, ethnographie, milieu ambiant et divertissement. Pour ce faire, il a tiré parti des éléments du passé-à l'instar des vestiges de la structure d'acier originale et des murs de pierre de 4 m de haut- qui, complétés par une structure supérieure en fer, s'élèvent à l'instar d'un mirador. La forte dénivellation topographique et la pénétration dans la mer de la structure, évoquant l'ancienne cargue, donnent un caractère intrinsèque à un projet qui prolonge l'utilisation de ligne côtière, tout en offrant un nouveau lieu de promenade et de loisirs dominicaux.

Questo progetto, situato in una vecchia piattaforma di carico per minerali ferrosi nella ria di Viveiro, vuole dare nuova vita al paesaggio con un intervento che accomuna eredità industriale, etnografia, rispetto per l'ambiente e svago. A tale scopo sono stati utilizzati elementi preesistenti — come i resti della struttura originale in acciaio e i muri di pietra alti 4 m — che, uniti a una struttura superiore in ferro, formano un belvedere. Il notevole dislivello topografico e l'addentramento nel mare della struttura che evoca la vecchia piattaforma aumentano il valore intrinseco di un progetto che riesce a dare un uso omogeneo alla linea della costa e a offrire un nuovo spazio per il passeggio e il relax domenicale.

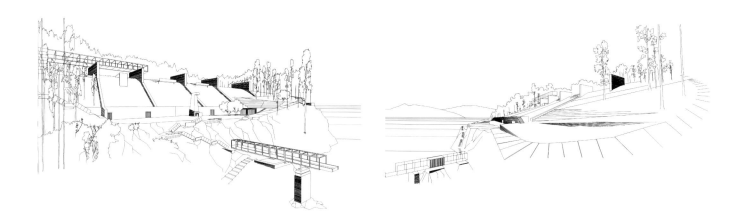

GERMÁN DEL SOL | SANTIAGO, CHILE

Website	www.germandelsol.cl
Project	Geometric Hot Springs
Location	Pucón, Chile
Year of completion	2003
Materials	chilean coigue wood, concrete, flat stones, trunks
Photo credits	Guy Wenborne

Located between the wild underbrush of the Villarrica National Park in the Andean Mountain chain, the De Sol intervention is full of poetic touches, in addition to respecting the environment. The thermal springs make use of over sixty water sources that shoot out at 176 °F with a flow of 4 gallons per second. They've facilitated its usage by constructing 20 bathing areas throughout a 1,500 foot Chilean coigue wood walkway that has been tinted red. The structure presents a continuous progression without steps and includes terraces from which one can enjoy the views of the natural surroundings. The installations also offer bath and changing rooms.

Mitten in der unberührten Natur des Parque Nacional de Villarica in den Anden entstanden diese Thermen von Del Sol – eine poetische Konstruktion, die respektvoll mit der Natur umgeht. Über sechzig Heißwasserquellen schießen hier mit 80 °C und einer Wassermenge von 15 Litern pro Sekunde aus dem Boden. Um diese auszunutzen, schuf man 20 Badebereiche entlang eines 450 Meter langen Laufstegs aus rot gefärbtem Coihue-Holz. Der durchgehende Laufsteg wird von Terrassen gesäumt, von denen aus man den Blick auf die wundervolle Umgebung genießen kann. Ebenso gibt es Bäder und Ankleidekabinen in den Thermen.

Situada entre la maleza brutal del Parque Nacional de Villarrica, en la Cordillera Andina, la intervención de Del Sol, aparte de ser respetuosa con el entorno, se hincha de tintes poéticos. Las termas aprovechan más de sesenta fuentes de agua que brotan a 80 °C y con un caudal de 15 litros por segundo. Para facilitar su uso se proyectaron 20 zonas de baño a lo largo de los 450 m que mide la pasarela de madera de coihué, teñida de rojo. La estructura presenta una progresión continua sin eslabones y se ve secundada con terrazas, desde donde se disfrutan las vistas del entorno natural. El emplazamiento ofrece también baños y vestidores.

Située entre les immenses sous-bois du Parc National de Villarrica, dans la cordillère des Andes, le projet de Del Sol, tout en respectant l'environnement, foisonne de touches poétiques. Les thermes disposent de plus de soixante sources d'eau chaude qui jaillissent à 80 °C avec un débit de 15 litres par seconde. Pour en faciliter l'utilisation, 20 zones de bains ont été installées le long des 450 m de la passerelle en bois de coigüe, teinte en rouge. La structure affiche une continuité fluide sans chaînons, dotée d'une série de terrasses d'où l'on peut jouir de vues sur l'environnement naturel. L'emplacement accueille aussi salles de bains et vestiaires.

Realizzato in mezzo alla natura selvaggia del Parco Nazionale di Villarica, nella cordigliera delle Ande, l'intervento di De Sol, oltre a rispettare l'ambiente, si tinge di sfumature poetiche. Le terme utilizzano più di sessanta sorgenti d'acqua calda, che sgorga a una temperatura di 80 °C e con una portata di 15 litri al secondo. Per facilitarne l'uso sono state create 20 zone da bagno lungo i 450 m di lunghezza di una passerella in legno di Coihué dipinta di rosso. La struttura, che si presenta come una progressione ininterrotta, dispone di terrazze – da dove si può godere della vista dei dintorni –, di bagni e di spogliatoi.

GLAßER & DAGENBACH | BERLIN, GERMANY

Website	www.glada-berlin.de
Project	Berlin Moabit Prison Historical Park
Location	Berlin, Germany
Year of completion	2006
Materials	concrete, 150 years old bricks
Photo credits	Udo Dagenbach
Illustration	Alexander Khomiakov

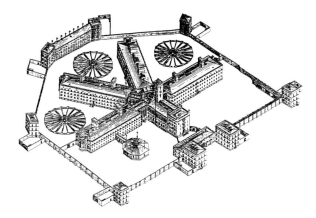

Berlin has regained this new green space that was used as a prison for 150 years. The construction –which is half-memorial, half leisure space– was developed while respecting the old structures and redesigning some of its parts in a contemporary fashion. After demolishing the majority of the buildings in the penitentiary complex, between 1956 and 1958, they built over 16 ft. high enclosure walls and created a recreational area inside which contrasts with the closed and afflictive nature that it once had. All of the concrete surfaces were painted earthen tones, which recalls the mortar used in brick masonry. The roughness of the surfaces makes direct reference to the grave and rough character of the prison.

Auf diesem Gelände in Berlin, wo sich 150 Jahre lang ein Gefängnis befand, wurde eine neue Grünzone geschaffen. Die Anlage ist eine Kombination aus Gedenkstätte und Freizeitzone. Manche der alten Strukturen blieben erhalten, und andere wurden teilweise modern umgestaltet. Nach dem Abriss der meisten Gefängnisgebäude zwischen 1956 und 1958 blieben die 5 Meter hohen Umfassungsmauern stehen. Innerhalb dieser Mauern schuf man eine Freizeitanlage, die einen Kontrast zu dem einst geschlossenen und schwermütigen Charakter des Ortes bildet. Alle Betonflächen haben Erdfarben wie der Mörtel, der einst für die Backsteinmauern benutzt wurde. Die rauen Oberflächen sind eine Anspielung auf die strenge Gefängnisumgebung.

Berlín recupera este nuevo espacio verde ocupado por una prisión durante 150 años. La obra –monumento conmemorativo y espacio para el ocio– se ha desarrollado respetando las antiguas estructuras o rediseñando de forma contemporánea algunas de sus partes. Tras la demolición de la mayoría de los edificios del complejo penitenciario, entre 1956 y 1958, se parte de los muros de cerramiento de 5 m de altura y se crea un espacio interior recreativo, que contrasta con el carácter cerrado y aflictivo que anteriormente se le dio a este enclave. Todas las superficies de hormigón son de color tierra, lo que recuerda al mortero usado para la mampostería de ladrillo. La rugosidad de dichas superficies remite directamente al tono grave y áspero del penal.

Berlin récupère ce nouvel espace vert occupé pendant 150 ans par une prison. L'ouvrage –mi mémorial, mi espace de loisirs– a été réalisé en respectant les anciennes structures ou en redessinant de façon contemporaine certains de ses éléments. Après la démolition de la majeure partie des édifices du complexe pénitencier, entre 1956 et 1958, on a créé, à partir des murs d'enceinte de 5 m de haut, un espace intérieur récréatif qui contraste avec le caractère fermé et attristant de l'ancienne enclave. Toutes les superficies en béton sont couleur terre, rappelant le mortier utilisé pour la maçonnerie en brique. La rugosité de ces superficies renvoie directement au système pénal pour son âpreté et sa gravité.

Berlino recupera questo spazio verde occupato per 150 anni da una prigione. L'opera — a metà tra monumento commemorativo e spazio dedicato all'ozio — è stata realizzata conservando le vecchie strutture o rimodellando alcune loro parti in stile contemporaneo. A seguito della demolizione della maggior parte degli edifici del complesso penitenziario tra il 1956 e il 1958, sono stati utilizzati i muri perimetrali alti 5 m per creare, al loro interno, uno spazio ricreativo che contrasta con il carattere chiuso e angoscioso che possedeva questo spazio in precedenza. Tutte le superfici di cemento sono in color terra, che ricorda la malta usata per la muratura in mattoni. La rugosità di queste superfici è un riferimento all'atmosfera opprimente e rigida della prigione.

...EID, DAS DIES... ...ERFÜLLT, IST UNTER MAUERWERK UND EISENGITTERN EIN HAUCH LEBENDIG, EINGEHEIMES ZITTERN

GLOBAL ARQUITECTURA PAISAGISTA | LISBOA, PORTUGAL

Website	www.gap.pt
Project	São Vicente's Caves Park
Location	São Vicente, Madeira, Portugal
Year of completion	2004
Materials	concrete, wood, corten steel, basalt stone
Photo credits	Leonardo Finotti

In this project the presence of a waterfall and cliff give a dramatic and naturalistic tone to an often frequented public area. The park forms part of the Volcano Center complex and serves as a platform towards the Atlantic Ocean which is just a few miles down the river if you follow the course of the Ribeira de São Vicente. The space is arranged around terraces –fruit of the terrain's previous exploitation– by way of a zigzag wooden walkway. Water, a primary structural element in the complex's organization, appears in different forms: running, channeled or still in tiny damns.

Ein Wasserfall und eine Steilküste lassen diese stark besuchte, öffentliche Anlage dramatisch und sehr natürlich wirken. Der Park gehört zum Vulkanmuseum und dient als Plattform über dem atlantischen Ozean. Er liegt einige Kilometer flussabwärts am Flussufer von São Vicente. Der Raum wird von zwei Terrassen, die früher dem Anbau dienten, und einer zickzackförmigen Holzplattform gegliedert. Das Wasser, wichtigstes Strukturelement des Geländes, taucht in verschiedenen Formen auf, als fließendes Wasser, in Kanälen oder in kleinen Seen gestaut.

La presencia de una cascada y un acantilado inspira el tono dramático y naturalístico de este proyecto, para un espacio público notablemente frecuentado. El parque es parte del complejo del Museo de la Volcanología y sirve de plataforma hacia el océano Atlántico, situado a unos pocos kilómetros río abajo, siguiendo el curso de la Ribeira de São Vicente. El espacio se articula a base de terrazas –herencia de una explotación anterior del terreno– con una pasarela de madera que se desliza en forma de zig-zag. El agua, elemento estructural primordial en la organización del conjunto, aparece en diferentes formas: corriente, canalizada o estancada en pequeños embalses.

La présence d'une cascade et d'une falaise insuffle un ton dramatique et naturaliste à ce projet de création d'un espace public fortement fréquenté. Le parc fait partie du complexe du Musée de la Volcanologie et sert de plateforme vers l'océan Atlantique, situé à quelques kilomètres en contrebas, suivant le cours de la Ribeira de São Vicente. L'espace s'articule autour de terrasses –héritage d'une exploitation antérieure du terrain– avec une passerelle en bois qui se faufile en zigzag. L'eau, élément structurel primordial dans l'organisation de l'ensemble, adopte diverses formes : courante, canalisée ou retenue dans des petits réservoirs.

Una cascata e una scogliera ispirano il tono drammatico e naturalista di questo progetto di uno spazio pubblico molto frequentato. Il parco forma parte del complesso del Museo di Vulcanologia e è una piattaforma aperta verso l'oceano Atlantico, che si trova pochi chilometri più avanti lungo il corso del fiume e la Ribeira de São Vicente. Lo spazio è organizzato su terrazze — eredità di un precedente sfruttamento del terreno — e è solcato a zigzag da una passerella in legno. L'acqua, elemento strutturante fondamentale nell'organizzazione del parco, si presenta in forme diverse: corrente, canalizzata o racchiusa in piccoli stagni.

GORA ART&LANDSCAPE | MALMÖ, SWEDEN

Website	www.gora.se
Project	Traffic Junction Odenskog
Location	Östersund, Sweden
Year of completion	2007
Materials	fibreglass, polyester, plastic
Photo credits	Lennart Jonasson

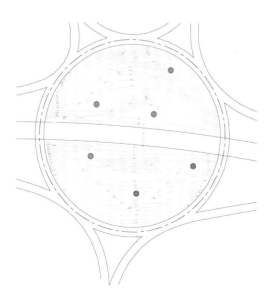

This rotunda has become the main expressive landscape reference in Odenskog, an industrial area under the administrative jurisdiction of Östersund. In order to highlight its relevance –a rotunda with a 459 ft. diameter– they've built low benches and planted rows of Amelanchier Spicata. The asymmetrical nature of the furniture and species planted go perfectly with the asymmetry represented by these small turquoise blue luminous sculptures. These floodlights, made with polyester reinforced with fiberglass, look opaque and solid during the day, while at night they delight drivers with their shiny, semi-transparent appearance.

Dieser Kreisverkehr mit Parkanlage ist zu einem wichtigen landschaftlichen Element in Odenskog, einem Industriegebiet in der Gemeinde Östersund, geworden. Um dem Kreisverkehr mit einem Durchmesser von 140 m einen eigenen Charakter zu geben, wurden niedrige Bänke aufgestellt und Reihen von Ähren-Felsenbirnen (Amelanchier Spicata) gepflanzt. Die asymmetrische Anordnung des Mobiliars und der Pflanzen passt perfekt zu der Asymmetrie der kleinen, türkisblauen Lichtskulpturen. Diese Lichtquellen aus mit Glasfaser verstärktem Polyester wirken tagsüber undurchsichtig und fest, nachts jedoch sehen sie halbtransparent und glänzend aus.

Esta rotonda se ha convertido en la principal referencia plástica y paisajística de Odenskog, una zona industrial perteneciente administrativamente a Östersund. Para subrayar la relevancia del emplazamiento –una rotonda de 140 m de diámetro– se han levantado bancos de baja altura y se han plantado bandas de Amelanchier Spicata. La disposición asimétrica de mobiliario y especies plantadas calza perfectamente con la asimetría representada por estas pequeñas esculturas lumínicas de color azul turquesa. Estos focos luminosos, forjados a base de poliéster reforzado con fibra de vidrio, se muestran opacos y de apariencia sólida durante el día, mientras que por la noche deleitan al conductor con su aspecto semitransparente y brillante.

Cette rotonde est devenue la principale référence plastique et paysagère d'Odenskog, zone industrielle relevant de l'administration d'Östersund. Pour souligner l'importance de l'emplacement –une rotonde de 140 m de diamètre– on a installé des bancs assez bas et planté des rangées d'Amelanchier Spicata. La disposition asymétrique du mobilier et des espèces plantées épouse parfaitement l'asymétrie représentée par ces petites sculptures lumineuses bleu turquoise. Ces foyers lumineux, forgés en polyester renforcé de fibre de verre, paraissent opaques et solides pendant la journée, alors que la nuit, ils charment le conducteur de leur aspect semi transparent et brillant.

Questa rotonda è diventata il principale punto di riferimento plastico e paesaggistico di Odenskog, una zona industriale che appartiene amministrativamente a Östersund. Al fine di sottolinearne l'importanza – il diametro della rotonda misura 140 m –, sono state collocate nel sito alcune panchine basse e sono stati piantati vari esemplari di Amelanchier Spicata. La disposizione asimmetrica degli arredi urbani e le specie di piante scelte si sposano alla perfezione con l'asimmetria delle piccole sculture luminose di color turchese. Questi punti luce, in poliestere rinforzato con fibra di vetro, presentano un aspetto solido e opaco durante il giorno, ma di notte stupiscono i conducenti diventando semitrasparenti e brillanti.

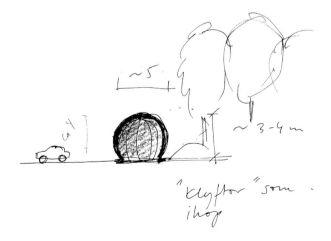

~5

~3-4 m

"klyftor" som
ihop

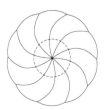

GUALLART ARCHITECTS | BARCELONA, SPAIN

Website	www.guallart.com
Project	Vinaròs Microcoasts
Location	Vinaròs, Spain
Year of completion	2006
Materials	wood
Photo credits	Nuria Díaz

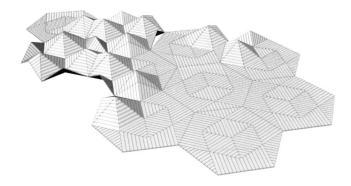

Located on the Paseo de la Ribera in Vinaròs, the Microcoasts represent artificial wooden islands on a part of the Mediterranean coast where constructions tend to use materials like brick and concrete. They chose wood since it's the stereotypical material used in naval architecture and because its width resists eventual fluctuations and floods. The hexagonal geometry of the Microcoasts is inspired on the studies of mathematician Benoît B. Mandelbrot. The result, which permits users free usage of the space without constructing on it, can be understood on two levels: on a large scale, the satisfaction of leisure time spent looking at the Mediterranean; and to a lesser degree, to admire miniscule coasts against the backdrop of the immense sea.

Die Microcostas an der Meerespromenade von Vinaroz sind künstliche Inseln aus Holz. Sie bilden einen Gegensatz zu den typischen Stein- und Betonkonstruktionen am Mittelmeer. Man wählte Holz als das typische Material, das im Schiffbau verwendet wird, und weil es aufgrund seiner Dicke eventuellen Schwankungen des Meeresspiegels und Überflutungen widersteht. Die hexagonalen Formen der Microcostas sind von den Studien des Mathematikers Benoît B. Mandelbrot inspiriert. So entstanden Strukturen, die eine Benutzung des Raums ohne eine feste Bebauung möglich machen und die man auf zweifache Weise verstehen kann. Zum einem kann man von ihnen aus das Mittelmeer genießen, zum anderen bilden sie bewundernswerte, winzige Küsten vor dem riesigen Meer.

Ubicadas en el Paseo de la Ribera de Vinaròs, las Microcostas representan islas artificiales de madera, dispuestas en una línea del litoral mediterráneo tradicionalmente atestado de construcción de ladrillo y hormigón. Se ha apostado por la madera ya que responde al estereotipo del material usado para la arquitectura naval y porque su espesor resiste eventuales fluctuaciones e inundaciones. La geometría hexagonal de las Microcostas se inspira en los estudios del matemático Benoît B. Mandelbrot. El resultado, que permite al usuario una apropiación libre del espacio sin urbanizarlo, expele una doble lectura: a gran escala, la satisfacción que provoca recrearse de cara al Mediterráneo; en menor grado, admirar unas costas minúsculas frente a la inmensidad del mar.

Situées sur le Paseo de la Ribera de Vinaròs, les « Microcostas » représentent des îles artificielles en bois, disposées le long du littoral méditerranéen, traditionnellement truffé de constructions en briques et béton. Les paysagistes ont opté pour le bois car il correspond au stéréotype du matériau utilisé pour l'architecture navale. En outre, son épaisseur résiste aux fluctuations et inondations éventuelles. La géométrie hexagonale des « Microcostas » s'inspire des études du mathématicien Benoît B. Mandelbrot. Le résultat, permettant à l'usager de s'approprier l'espace libre sans l'urbaniser, suggère une double lecture : d'abord, la satisfaction que l'on ressent à se reposer face à la Méditerranée, ensuite, la possibilité de contempler les côtes minuscules face à l'immensité de la mer.

Situate lungo il Paseo de la Ribera de Vinaròs, le Micorcoste sono isole artificiali in legno, disposte su una parte del litorale mediterraneo tradizionalmente gremita di costruzioni in mattoni e cemento. È stato scelto il legno in quanto risponde allo stereotipo del materiale usato nell'architettura navale e perché, grazie al suo spessore, è capace di resistere alle fluttuazioni del livello dell'acqua e alle inondazioni. La geometria esagonale delle Microcoste si ispira agli studi del matematico Benoît B. Mandelbrot. Il progetto, che permette di appropriarsi di uno spazio senza urbanizzarlo, offre una duplice lettura: da una parte, la soddisfazione di potersi rilassare di fronte al Mediterraneo, dall'altra, la possibilità di ammirare coste minuscole davanti all'immensità del mare.

GUALTIERO OBERTI | AZZONICA DI SORISOLE, ITALY

Project   Fluvial Park of Cunella
Location   Cunella, Italy
Year of completition 2007
Materials   concrete colored in paste with natural oxides for
                   the strucures, stabilized chopped gravel for the flooring
Photo credits   Gualtiero Oberti

The construction of this fluvial park has instilled order in a space that was being used as a spontaneous meeting point and recreation area in the summer. The project was based on two concepts: nature and a rational design based on mathematics. The smooth, sinuous lines of the park are inspired on organic shapes; they've sought to establish a new dialogue with nature. Although they've included a parking area, the principal elements are the barbeques and the fountain. The material used, cement colored with metallic oxides to achieve an ochre color, contrast with the greens and browns in its surroundings.

Durch die Anlage dieses Flussparks wurde eine Landschaft geordnet, die in den Sommermonaten bereits als Treffpunkt und Ort der Erholung diente. Die Planung basierte auf zwei Konzepten, auf der Natur und einer rationellen, von der Mathematik bestimmten Gestaltung. Die sanften, kurvigen Linien des Parks sind von organischen Formen inspiriert, durch die ein neuer Dialog mit der Natur entstehen sollte. Obwohl auch ein Parkplatz angelegt wurde, sind die wichtigsten Elemente die Grillplätze und ein Brunnen. Durch den verwendeten, mit Oxiden eingefärbten Zement entstand eine Ockerfarbe, die einen Kontrast zu den Grün- und Brauntönen der Umgebung bildet.

La construcción de este parque fluvial ha supuesto la ordenación de un espacio que ya estaba siendo utilizado de forma espontánea como lugar de reunión y recreo durante los meses de verano. El proyecto se ha cimentado en dos conceptos: la naturaleza y el diseño racional basado en las matemáticas. Las suaves y sinuosas líneas del parque se inspiran en formas orgánicas; se ha buscado establecer un nuevo diálogo con la naturaleza. Aunque se ha habilitado una zona de aparcamiento, los elementos principales del conjunto son unas barbacoas y una fuente. El material utilizado, cemento coloreado con óxidos metálicos para conseguir un tono ocre, contrasta con los colores verdes y marrones del entorno.

La construction de ce parc en rive de fleuve a supposé l'ordonnance d'un espace qui était déjà utilisé de façon spontanée comme lieu de rencontre et de loisir pendant l'été. Le projet se base sur deux concepts : la nature d'une part, et le design tant rationnel que mathématique d'autre part. Les lignes douces et sinueuses du parc sont inspirées des formes organiques, par lesquelles un nouveau dialogue avec la nature a été recherché. Bien qu'une zone de parking ait été aménagée, les éléments principaux de l'ensemble sont des barbecues et un jeu d'eau. Le matériel utilisé, un ciment coloré par des oxydes de métal afin de lui conférer un ton ocre, contraste avec les verts et bruns qui l'entourent.

La costruzione di questo parco fluviale ha riordinato uno spazio utilizzato in precedenza come luogo di ritrovo e svago durante l'estate. Il progetto fa perno su due concetti: la natura e un design razionale basato sulla matematica. Le linee dolci e sinuose del parco traggono ispirazione da forme organiche e cercano di stabilire un dialogo con la natura. Sebbene sia stata adibita un'area a parcheggio, gli elementi principali dell'intervento sono i barbecue e la fontana. Il materiale utilizzato, cemento combinato con ossidi metallici per ottenere un colore ocra, fa contrasto con il verde e il marrone dell'ambiente circostante.

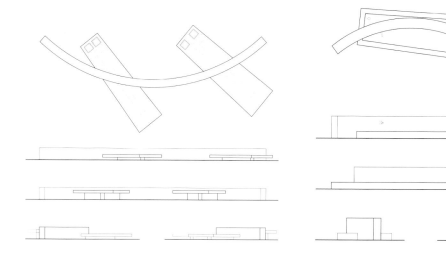

GUSTAFSON PORTER | LONDON, UK

Website	www.gustafson-porter.com
Project	Diana, Princess of Wales Memorial Fountain
Location	London, UK
Year of completion	2004
Materials	de lank granite
Photo credits	Helene Binet

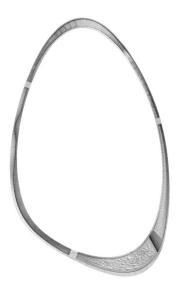

The design of this discreet, but symbolic, memorial to Lady Di is the result of intelligently fusing high-tech production techniques with the use of stone sculptors. To a certain extent, this blend of modern technologies and artisanal techniques represents the princess' character by combining sophisticated status with proximity to the working class. The memorial, located in London's Hyde Park, is distinguished by an oval shape in the middle of an open area. The project makes use of the area's typography to have water flow in two directions from a fountain located on the highest part of the oval perimeter. On the lowest point the waters reunite again and are pumped back to the original source in a cyclical fashion.

Die Gestaltung dieses diskreten, aber sehr symbolhaften Denkmals an Lady Di basiert auf der intelligenten Verbindung von Produktionstechniken. High-Tech wurde hier mit Steinhauerei verbunden. Diese Vermischung von modernen Techniken mit altem Kunsthandwerk repräsentiert auch auf eine gewisse Weise den Charakter der Prinzessin. Sie hatte einen gesellschaftlich hohen Stand inne und war dennoch dem einfachen Volk nah. Das Denkmal im Londoner Hyde Park fällt durch seine ovale Form inmitten der offenen Landschaft auf. Die Bodenform wurde dazu genutzt, Wasser vom höher gelegenen Teil des Ovals aus in zwei Richtungen fließen zu lassen. Am tiefsten Punkt treffen diese Strömungen wieder aufeinander und werden zurück zur Originalquelle gepumpt. So entsteht ein ewiger Zyklus.

El diseño de este monumento conmemorativo de la princesa Lady Di, discreto pero, al mismo tiempo, simbólico, responde a la inteligente fusión de técnicas de producción *high-tech* y el uso de escultores de piedra. Esta mezcla de tecnologías modernas con técnicas artesanales representa, en cierto modo, el carácter de la princesa, de estatus sofisticado pero de trato cercano al pueblo llano. El monumento, emplazado en el Hyde Park londinense, destaca por su forma oval en medio de una extensión abierta. El proyecto se sirve de la topografía del lugar para hacer fluir el agua en dos direcciones, a partir de una fuente situada en la parte más alta del perímetro ovalado. En el punto más bajo de éste se unen de nuevo las aguas y son bombeadas a la fuente original, repitiéndose así el ciclo eternamente.

Le design de ce mémorial à la fois discret et symbolique, érigé en souvenir de la princesse Lady Di, répond à la fusion intelligente entre techniques de production *high-tech* et emploi de sculptures de pierre. Ce mélange de technologies modernes et de techniques artisanales représente, d'une certaine manière, le caractère de la princesse, proche du peuple malgré son statut social. Le mémorial, situé dans Hyde Park, à Londres, se détache par sa forme ovale au cœur d'une extension ouverte. Le projet utilise la topographie du lieu pour laisser l'eau couler dans deux directions, à partir d'une source située dans la partie supérieure du périmètre ovale. Au point le plus bas, les eaux s'unissent à nouveau et sont pompées à la source originale, le cycle se répétant ainsi à l'infini.

Il disegno di questo monumento commemorativo della principessa Lady Di, discreto ma, al tempo stesso, simbolico, è il frutto della combinazione di tecniche di produzione *high-tech* con la lavorazione a mano della pietra, ad opera di scultori. Questa fusione di tecnologia moderna e tecniche artigianali esprime, in un certo senso, il carattere della principessa: sofisticata ma con un modo di fare che la avvicinava al popolo. Il monumento, situato all'interno di Hyde Park, a Londra, spicca per la sua forma ovale collocata al centro di uno spazio aperto. Il progetto sfrutta la topografia del luogo per far scorrere l'acqua, che sgorga da una fontana situata nella parte più alta del perimetro ovale, in due direzioni diverse. Nel punto più basso del perimetro i due rivoli tornano a congiungersi e l'acqua è pompata nuovamente alla fontana, facendo sì che il ciclo si ripeta indefinitamente.

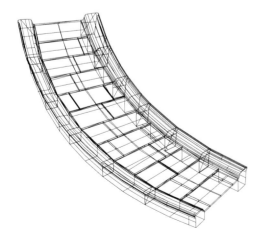

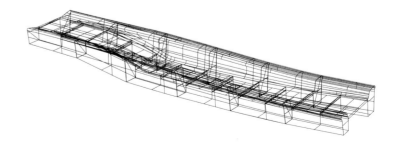

JENSEN & SKODVIN ARKITEKTKONTOR AS | OSLO, NORWAY

Website	www.jsa.no
Project	Gudbrandsjuvet Tourist Project
Location	Burtigard, Gudbrandsjuvet, Norway
Year of completion	2007
Materials	ordinary steel, stainless steel, concrete, glass
Photo credits	Jensen & Skodvin Arkitektkontor AS

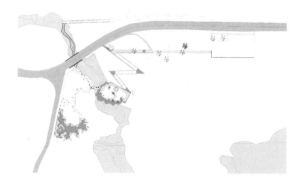

This walkway built along a segment of the Valldola River was intended for the tourist routes which, year after year, go from Geiranger Fjord to Trollstigen. This way, hundreds of thousands of tourists can enjoy the cascade of rough waters that occurs when glaciers melt in spring. The project incorporates platforms, bridges, a visitors' center and a *landscape* hotel run by one of the area's residents. The walkway, which is built above the area's rocky geography, combines sinuous steel and stainless steel parts, with a zigzag area made of concrete and glass.

Entlang eines Abschnitts des Flusses Valldola wurde für die touristischen Routen vom Fjord de Geiranger bis Trollstigen wurde diese Fußgängerbrücke errichtet. So können die vielen Touristen die Wasserfälle und die Wildbäche genießen, die jedes Jahr entstehen, wenn die Gletscher im Frühjahr schmelzen. Die Anlage besteht aus Plattformen, Brücken, einem Besucherzentrum und einem Landschaftshotel, das von einem Anwohner der Region betrieben wird. Die Fußgängerbrücke schwebt über dem unebenen, felsigen Gelände und kombiniert kurvige Abschnitte aus Stahl und Edelstahl mit geraderen Abschnitten aus Beton und Glas.

Esta pasarela erigida a lo largo de un tramo del río Valldøla ha sido construida para las rutas turísticas que, año tras año, tienen lugar del Fjord de Geiranger a Trollstigen. De esta forma, los cientos de miles de turistas pueden disfrutar de las cascadas y las aguas bravas generadas cuando los glaciares se funden en primavera. El proyecto incorpora plataformas, puentes, un centro de visitantes y un *landscape* hotel impulsado por un residente de la zona. La pasarela, que se alza en voladizo por encima de la accidentada geografía rocosa del lugar, combina tramos sinuosos de acero y acero inoxidable, así como trechos de silueta sesgada a base de hormigón y vidrio.

Cette passerelle érigée le long d'un bras du fleuve Valldøla a été construite pour les itinéraires touristiques qui, chaque année, amènent au Fjord de Geiranger à Trollstigen. Ainsi, des centaines de milliers de touristes peuvent jouir des cascades et des eaux sauvages issues de la fonte des glaciers au printemps. Le projet comprend des plateformes, des ponts, un centre de visiteur et un hôtel *paysagé*, à l'initiative d'un résident de la zone. La passerelle, qui s'élève en saillie au-dessus de la géographie accidentée et rocheuse du site, conjugue bras sinueux d'acier et acier inoxydable et ébauches de silhouettes tordues en béton et verre.

Questa passerella, situata lungo un tratto del fiume Valldøla, è stata costruita per arricchire l'itinerario turistico che, anno dopo anno, conduce centinaia di migliaia di turisti dal fiordo di Geiranger a Trollstigen, facendo sì che possano godere della vista delle cascate e delle acque in tempesta, frutto dello scioglimento dei ghiacciai in primavera. Il progetto prevede piattaforme, ponti, un centro per i visitatori e un *landscape* hotel, la cui costruzione è stata fomentata da un residente della zona. La passerella, che si protende in aggetto al di sopra dell'irregolare geografia rocciosa del luogo, combina tratti dalle forme sinuose in acciaio e in acciaio inossidabile con tratti dal contorno spigoloso in cemento e vetro.

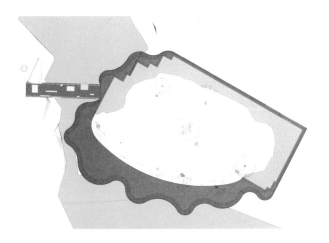

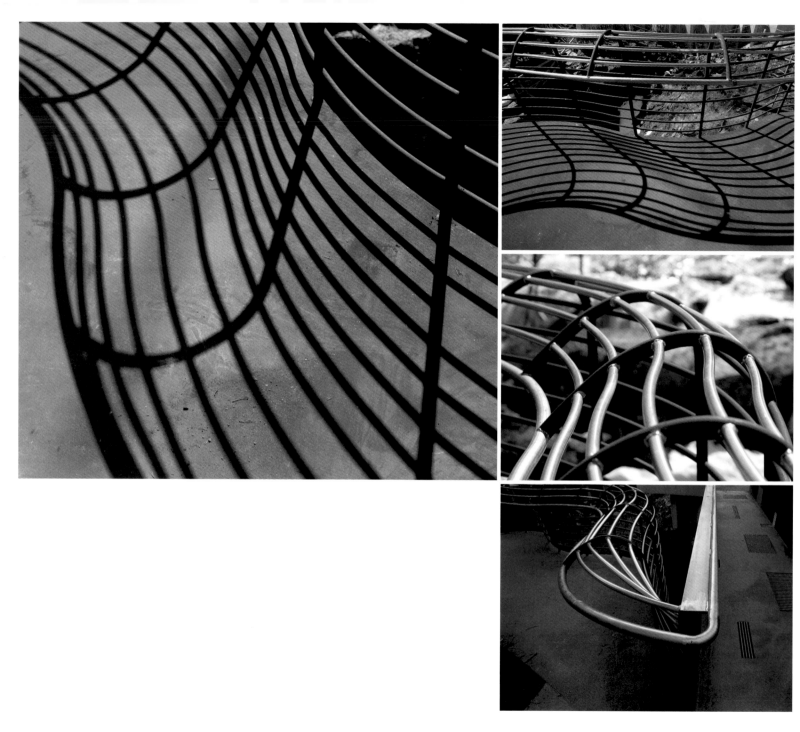

KARRES EN BRANDS LANDSCHAPSARCHITECTEN | HILVERSUM, THE NETHERLANDS

Website	www.karresenbrands.nl
Project	De Nieuwe Ooster Cemetery
Location	Amsterdam, The Netherlands
Year of completion	2006 (1st stage)
Materials	zinc, prefabricated concrete, terrazzo finish
Photo credits	Karres en Brands Landschapsarchitecten bv, Peter Zoech

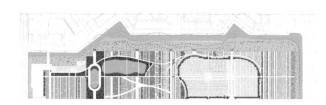

The projected extension of this cemetery represents juxtaposition between the collective and the individual, and is a response to the different demands that have been made in recent years in relation to the death-burial-memory trinomial. In contrast with the original buildings planned by Springer in 1889, the new constructions seek to form a set without a defined structure or identity, as if they were disjointed fragments. The Hilversum Studio decided on giving each of the three new areas its own character: water, a wall to mark off the area for coffins and an area for ashes that is flanked by parterres. The second phase will be completed in 2008.

Dieser Friedhof wurde so angelegt, dass er eine Nebeneinanderstellung des Kollektiven und des Individuellen darstellt und eine Antwort auf die verschiedenen Notwendigkeiten, die in den letzten Jahren in Bezug auf das Trinom Tod - Bestattung - Erinnerung entstanden sind. Den ursprünglichen Anlagen, die Springer 1889 plante, wurde ein neuer Teil gegenübergestellt, der keine definierte Struktur und Identität hat und deshalb wie eine Ansammlung auseinanderfallender Fragmente wirkt. Das Planungsstudio Hilversum hat jeder der drei neuen Zonen einen anderen Charakter gegeben. Diese Zonen sind das Wasser, die Mauer, die die Räume mit den Särgen begrenzt, und die Zone der Urnen, die von Blumenbeeten gesäumt ist. Die zweite Bauphase wird 2008 fertiggestellt.

La extensión proyectada de este cementerio representa la yuxtaposición entre lo colectivo y lo individual, y una respuesta decidida a las diferentes demandas surgidas en los últimos años en relación con el trinomio defunción-entierro-memoria. En contraposición con las dependencias originales del emplazamiento, planeadas por Springer en 1889, las partes nuevas del enclave abogan por un conjunto sin una estructura e identidad definidas, como si de fragmentos desencajados se tratase. El estudio de Hilversum ha decidido apostar por un carácter diferente para cada una de las tres nuevas zonas: el agua, el muro que delimita las dependencias para los ataúdes y la zona de deposición de cenizas, flanqueada por parterres. La segunda fase será completada en 2008.

L'extension de ce cimetière représente la juxtaposition entre le collectif et l'individuel. C'est une réponse claire aux différentes demandes surgies dans les dernières années par rapport au trinôme décès-enterrement-mémoire. Contrastant avec les dépendances originales du site, planifiées par Springer en 1889, les parties neuves de l'enclave plaident pour un ensemble sans structure, ni identité définies, comme s'il s'agissait de fragments déboîtés. L'étude de Hilversum a décidé donner un caractère différent à chacune des trois nouvelles zones : l'eau, le mur qui délimite les dépendances pour les cercueils et la zone de dépôt des cendres, ornée de parterres. La deuxième phase s'achèvera en 2008.

Il progetto di estensione di questo cimitero esprime la giustapposizione tra collettivo e individuale e è una risposta decisa alle domande che sono state poste, negli ultimi anni, in relazione al trinomio morte-sepoltura-memoria. In contrasto con le costruzioni originali, progettate da Springer nel 1889, le nuove costruzioni si presentano senza una struttura e un'identità definite, quasi si trattasse di frammenti sparsi. Lo studio Hilversum ha voluto infondere un carattere differente a ognuna delle tre nuove zone: l'acqua, il muro che delimita le costruzioni dove si alloggiano i feretri e la zona dove si conservano le ceneri, fiancheggiata da parterre. La seconda fase del progetto sarà terminata nel 2008.

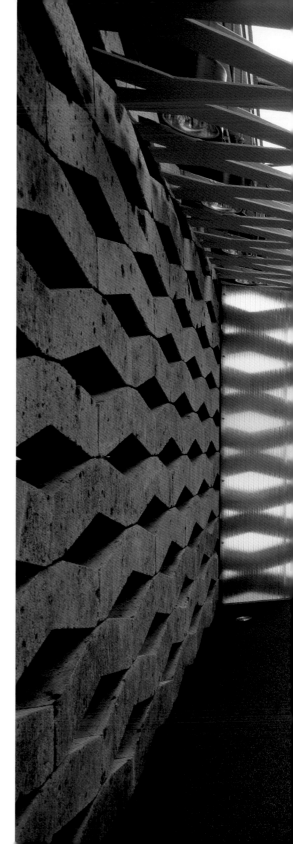

KENGO KUMA & ASSOCIATES | TOKYO, JAPAN

Website	www.kkaa.co.jp
Project	Chokkura Plaza & Shelter
Location	Takanezawa, Shioya-gun, Tochigi, Japan
Year of completion	2005
Materials	oya stone, stainless steel
Photo credits	Daici Ano

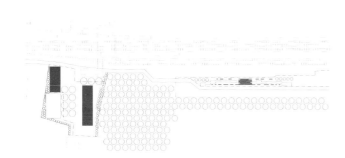

This is a two-headed project with a heavy organic accent. Chokkura Plaza, beside the Hoshakuji station, occupies the space where there was once a rice warehouse built with Oya stone. They chose this material for its great porosity and warm appearance, as it not only serves as a surface material but as one of the building's formal elements. Using this material to build the diagonal structure gives texture to the whole complex. 330 ft. away one finds the second part of the project: a park in an area with train tracks that take you to the plaza. In this case they preferred a light structure formed by a virtually transparent stainless steel net, which over the years will get covered by the creeper, Trumpet Honeysuckle.

Ein doppelköpfiges, sehr organisches Projekt. Der Platz Chokkura am Bahnhof Hoshakuji entstand dort, wo sich einst ein Reislager aus Oya-Stein befand. Man wählte auch für den Platz dieses Material, denn es ist porös und wirkt warm. So dient es nicht nur zur Verkleidung, sondern auch als Formelement des Gebäudes. Die diagonale Struktur aus diesem Material wirkt an allen Konstruktionen wie eine Textur. 100 Meter von diesem Standort entfernt befindet sich der zweite Teil der Anlage, ein Park in einer Zone mit Eisenbahnschienen, die zum Platz führen. Hier wählte man eine leichte Struktur aus einem transparenten Edelstahlnetz, das aber im Laufe der Zeit von einer Kletterpflanze der Art Trompeten-Geißblatt bedeckt wird.

Un proyecto bicéfalo con marcado acento orgánico. La Chokkura Plaza, vecina a la estación de Hoshakuji, ocupa el espacio donde antes se alzaba un almacén de arroz construido con piedra Oya. Se ha optado por usar este material por su alta porosidad y aspecto cálido, que funciona no sólo como revestimiento, sino como elemento formal del edificio. La estructura con este material, tramada en diagonal, aporta un viso de textura a todo el conjunto. A 100 m del emplazamiento se encuentra la segunda parte del proyecto: un parque en una zona ocupada por vías de ferrocarril que conducen a la plaza. En este caso se prefirió una estructura ligera, formada por una malla de acero inoxidable virtualmente transparente, que con los años será cubierta por una planta trepadora, la Trumpet Honeysuckle.

Un projet bicéphale aux forts accents organiques. La Chokkura Plaza, voisine de la station de Hoshakuji, occupe l'espace où, autrefois, s'élevait un magasin de riz construit en pierre Oya. Ce matériau a été choisi pour sa grande porosité et son aspect chaleureux, car hormis sa qualité de revêtement, c'est aussi un élément formel de l'édifice. La puissante structure de ce matériau, tramée en diagonale, confère à l'ensemble un aspect texturé. A 100 m du site, la deuxième partie du projet se déploie sous forme de parc dans une zone occupée par des voies de chemin de fer qui conduisent à la place. Ici, on a privilégié une structure légère formée par une maille d'acier inoxydable virtuellement transparente, qui au fil des ans, sera recouverte de plantes grimpantes, comme le chèvrefeuille trompette.

Un progetto bicefalo con uno spiccato carattere organico. Il Chokkura Plaza, vicino alla stazione di Hoshakuji, è stato costruito sullo spazio occupato in precedenza da un magazzino di riso in pietra Oya. Questo materiale è stato scelto per la sua alta porosità e per il suo aspetto confortevole, potendo essere impiegato sia come rivestimento, sia come elemento formale dell'edificio. Le pietre, disposte in diagonale, formano la trama esterna della struttura. A 100 m da questa, si trova la seconda parte del progetto: un parco situato in una zona occupata da binari del treno che conducono alla piazza. In questo caso si è preferito creare una struttura leggera, formata da una rete in acciaio inossidabile pressoché trasparente che, negli anni, sarà ricoperta da un rampicante, la Lonicera sempervirens.

187

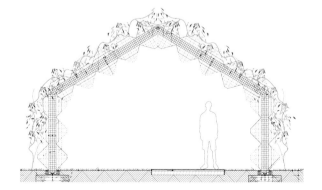

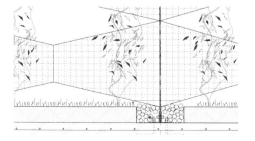

KRISTINE JENSENS TEGNESTUE | AARHUS, DENMARK

Website	www.kristinejensen.dk
Project	Prags Boulevard
Location	Copenhagen, Denmark
Year of completion	2005
Materials	asphalt, steel, wood, black rubber
Photo credits	Simon Høgsberg, Christina Capetillo

With its **1.2 miles** length and random relation between spaces for circulation, recreation and rest, Prags Boulevard represents one of the largest and most significant urban developments in Copenhagen in recent years. Different recreational areas (square, garden, stage, court, cage, kindergarten, ramp/skating area) alternate with the sculptural uniqueness of the Prag-Chairs, scattered with parterres. This individual chair model is "borrowed" from other European parks and plazas, but made to look like a film director's chair and with the word *prags* printed on the backrest. They've also expressly designed the Prager Lamp, a lamp with bright colors that embellishes and graphically emphasizes the boulevard's large trajectory. Pictography stands out in a project that combines urban design, graphic design and landscaping.

Der 2 km lange Prags Boulevard mit seiner wie zufällig wirkenden Abfolge von Durchgangs- und Erholungszonen ist einer der wichtigsten und größten Plätze Kopenhagens, die in den letzten Jahren angelegt wurden. Verschiedene Erholungszonen wechseln sich ab (Platz, Garten, Podium, Hof, Käfig, Kindergarten, Skaterampe). Auffallend sind die skulpturalen Sitzgelegenheiten, die Prag-Chairs, die überall verteilt sind. Es handelt sich um ein Einzelsitzmodell nach dem Vorbild anderer Parks und Plätze in Europa, die aber gleichzeitig einem Regisseurstuhl gleichen. Auf der Rückenlehne steht das Wort „Prags". Ebenso wurde eigens für den Boulevard die Prager Lamp entworfen, Straßenlaternen in lebhaften Farben, die den langen Boulevard säumen und verschönern. In diesem Projekt, das urbanes Design, Grafikdesign und Landschaftsplanung kombiniert, hebt sich vor allem die Piktographie ab.

Con sus 2 km de largo y la relación aleatoria de espacios para la circulación, recreación y reposo, Prags Boulevard representa una de las acciones urbanas más significativas y extensas de Copenhague en los últimos años. Se alternan las diferentes áreas recreativas (*square, garden, stage, court, cage, kindergarten, ramp/skating area*) con la singularidad escultural de las Prag-Chairs, esparcidas por los parterres. Se trata de un modelo de silla individual «prestado» de otros parques y plazas europeas, pero hecho a semejanza de la butaca de los directores de cine y con la palabra *prags* impresa en el respaldo trasero. También se ha diseñado expreso la Prager Lamp, una luminaria de tonos vivos que embellece y remarca gráficamente el largo trayecto dibujado por el boulevard. La pictografía destaca en un proyecto que combina diseño urbano, diseño gráfico y paisajismo.

Avec ses 2 km de long et la relation aléatoire des espaces de circulation, recréation et repos, le Boulevard de Prague représente une des interventions urbaines majeures et des plus étendues de Copenhague, de ces dernières années. Les différentes zones de recréations (*place, jardin, scène, patio, cage, jardin d'enfants, zone de rampe pour skate*) s'alternent avec les singulières « Chaises de Prague », éparpillées sur les parterres. Il s'agit d'un modèle de chaise individuelle « emprunté » aux autres places et parcs européens, mais réalisé sur le modèle des fauteuils des directeurs de cinéma avec le mot *prags* gravé à l'arrière. De même la « Prager Lamp » conçue pour l'occasion, est un liminaire aux tons vifs qui embellit et accentue graphiquement la longue trajectoire dessinée par le boulevard. La pictographie est exaltée dans un projet qui allie design urbain, design graphique et paysagisme.

Con i suoi 2 km di lunghezza e una relazione aleatoria tra spazi di circolazione, svago e riposo, il Prags Boulevard rappresenta uno degli interventi urbani più significativi e estesi nella Copenaghen degli ultimi anni. Le diverse zone di svago (*square, garden, stage, court, cage, kindergarten, ramp/skating area*) si alternano alla singolarità scultorea delle Prag-Chairs, sparse per i parterre. Si tratta di un modello di sedia individuale preso in prestito da altri parchi e piazze europee, ma fatto a somiglianza delle sedie dei registi e con la parola *prags* stampata sulla parte posteriore dello schienale. Di disegno esclusivo è anche la Prager Lamp, un lampione dalle tonalità vivaci che abbellisce e accentua il largo percorso tracciato dal boulevard. In un progetto che combina disegno urbano, disegno grafico e paesaggismo, risalta la pittografia.

KUHN TRUNINGER LANDSCHAFTSARCHITEKTEN | ZURICH, SWITZERLAND

Website	www.kuhntruninger.ch
Project	Weiach Cemetery
Location	Weiach, Switzerland
Year of completion	2004
Materials	concrete, bronze, larch wood
Photo credits	Ralph Feiner

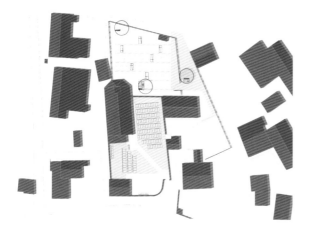

This extension of the old cemetery in this Swiss rural community perfectly fulfils two requirements: respect and transparency. Respect towards the old church-rectory-farm complex. Dating back to the early XVIIIth century and with its fortified walls from the wars between Protestants and Catholics preserved intact. And transparency because the new intervention, mainly arranged around the existing rectory and gardens, is developed over a 6 ft. alerce fence that can be seen though. They've also incorporated water elements and stone furniture from the region, as well as horizontal concrete memorial tablets with bronze crosses engraved in them.

Diese Erweiterung des alten Friedhofes einer ländlichen Gemeinde in der Schweiz vermittelt das, was gesucht wurde: Respekt und Transparenz. Der alte Gebäudekomplex (Kirche, Pfarrhaus Bauernhof) aus dem 18. Jh., der den Kriegen zwischen den Protestanten und Katholiken seine befestigten Mauern verdankt, wurde mit großem Respekt behandelt. Und die Transparenz erreichte man, indem man um das Pfarrhaus und die existierenden Gärten eine 2 m hohe Umzäunung aus Lärchenholz schuf, die den Blick frei lässt. Ebenso wurden Elemente aus Wasser und Mobiliar aus Steinen der Region gestaltet, und waagerechte Grabsteine aus Beton mit eingravierten Bronzekreuzen.

Esta extensión del antiguo cementerio de esta comunidad rural suiza cumple excelentemente dos requisitos: respeto y transparencia. Respeto al antiguo complejo iglesia-rectoría-granja, fechado a principios del siglo XVIII y mantenido intacto en sus muros fortificados y heredados de las guerras entre protestantes y católicos de aquella época. Y transparencia porque la nueva intervención, desplegada principalmente en torno a la rectoría y los jardines existentes, se desarrolla sobre una valla de alerce de 2 m, que permite la visibilidad a través de ésta. Se han incorporado también elementos de agua y mobiliario de piedra de la región, así como lápidas horizontales de hormigón gravadas con cruces de bronce.

L'extension de cet ancien cimetière d'une communauté rurale suisse remplit à merveilles deux exigences : respect et transparence. Respect de l'ancien complexe église-cure-grange, datant du début du XVIIIe siècle et resté intact entre ses murs fortifiés, hérités des guerres entre protestants et catholiques de cette époque. Transparence parce que la nouvelle intervention, qui se déploie essentiellement autour de la cure et des jardins existants, se développe sur une vallée de cèdres de 2 m, permettant une visibilité toute en transparence ce projet intègre également des éléments aquatiques et de mobilier en pierre de la région, ainsi que des blocs horizontaux en béton, gravés de croix de bronze.

L'estensione dell'antico cimitero di questa comunità rurale svizzera soddisfa pienamente due requisiti: rispetto e trasparenza. Rispetto per l'antico complesso chiesa-casa del parroco-stalla, degli inizi del XVIII secolo, mantenuto intatto dalle mura fortificate eredità della guerra dell'epoca tra protestanti e cattolici. E trasparenza, perché il nuovo intervento, concentrato principalmente sulla casa del parroco e sui giardini esistenti, si sviluppa intorno a una recinzione in larice di 2 m che permette di vedere al di là di essa. Il progetto accoglie altri elementi, come acqua, arredi urbani in pietra della regione e lapidi orizzontali in cemento con croci in bronzo.

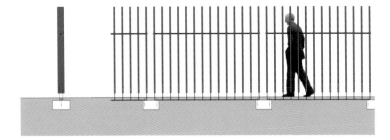

LANDWORKS STUDIO | BOSTON, USA

Website	www.landworks-studio.com
Project	Court Square Press Courtyard
Location	South Boston, Massachusetts, USA
Year of completion	2003
Materials	ipe, aluminium
Photo credits	Landworks Studio Inc

Located in the atrium of the Court Square building which dates back to 1906, its design is soaked in the enclave's post-industrial past. The aim was to create an urban oasis that combines a series of elements that used to be conflictive: the inert and organic materiality, its rough and refined texture and the transition between light and dark. They used a choreography formed by overlapping layers, deliberately seeking to organize the space so as to offer a fragmented view of it. This makes the lighting system stand out –which includes lit benches with windows– the winding silhouette of the wooden and steel walkway, and the bamboo plantation's textural animation, which uses inserted fiber optics. During the day, this structural material produces lines and shadows over the bamboo layer.

Im Atrium des Gebäudes Court Square aus dem Jahr 1906 unterstrich man mit der Gestaltung den postindustriellen Charakter der Zone. Es sollte ein Stadtoase entstehen, die Elemente kombiniert, die früher Gegensätze bildeten: die organische und leblose Gegenständlichkeit, die raue und die feine Textur und der Übergang von Licht zu Dunkel. Die Planer organisierten den Raum wie eine Choreographie aus übereinander gelagerten Schichten, so als ob eine zerlegte Ansicht dieser Strukturierung selbst gezeigt würde. Auffallend ist das Beleuchtungssystem (u. a. leuchtende Bänke mit Fenstern), entstanden durch das Einfügen von Glasfaserstreifen. Ebenso schön sind die geschlängelte Silhouette des Laufstegs aus Holz und Stahl und die Textur der Bambuspflanzung. Tagsüber produziert die Struktur Linien und Schatten auf der Bambusschicht.

Ubicado en el atrio del edificio Court Square, que data de 1906, el diseño se empapa del legado postindustrial del enclave. El objetivo era crear un oasis urbano que combinara una serie de elementos otrora confrontados: la materialidad orgánica e inerte, la textura de lo áspero y refinado y la transición entre lo luminoso y lo oscuro. A modo de coreografía formada por capas sobrepuestas, se buscó deliberadamente una organización del espacio que ofreciese una visión fragmentada del mismo. Así destacan el sistema de iluminación –que incluye bancos luminosos con ventanas–, la silueta serpenteada de la pasarela de madera y acero y la animación textural de la plantación de bambú, mediante la inserción de bandas de fibra óptica. Durante el día, este tejido estructural produce líneas y sombras sobre la capa de bambú.

Situé dans l'édifice Court Square, datant de 1906, le design s'imprègne de l'héritage post-industriel de l'enclave. L'objectif est de créer une oasis urbaine qui combine une série d'éléments opposés : la matérialité organique et inerte, la texture de ce qui est âpre et raffiné et la transition entre lumière et obscurité. A l'instar d'une chorégraphie composée de couches superposées, la conception cherche délibérément une organisation de l'espace qui en offre une vision fragmentée. Le système d'éclairage –comprenant des bancs lumineux dotés de fenêtres–, la silhouette sinueuse de la passerelle en bois et acier et l'animation texturée de la plantation de bambou, sont mis en évidence grâce à l'insertion de bandes de fibre optique. Dans la journée, ce tissu structurel crée des lignes et des ombres sur la couche de bambou.

Situato nell'atrio dell'edificio Court Square, datato 1906, questo progetto è intriso dall'eredità industriale del sito. L'obiettivo è stato quello di creare un'oasi urbana in cui si fondessero elementi una volta considerati antitetici: la materialità organica e inerte, le superfici ruvide e levigate, la transizione tra la luce e l'oscurità. Come una coreografia formata da strati sovrapposti, si è cercata deliberatamente un'organizzazione dello spazio che offrisse una visione frammentata dello stesso. Spiccano il sistema di illuminazione — che include panche luminose con finestre —, il profilo ondulato della passerella in legno e acciaio e la texture animata prodotta dalle canne di bambù in cui sono state inserite fibre ottiche. Di giorno, questo tessuto strutturale produce linee e ombre sul bambù.

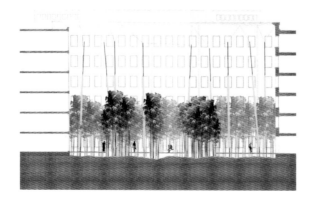

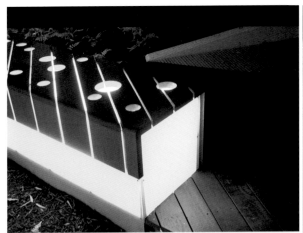

MCGREGOR & PARTNERS | SYDNEY, AUSTRALIA

Website	www.mcgregorpartners.com.au
Project	Form/Lot 302
Location	Zetland, Sydney, Australia
Year of completion	2003
Materials	concrete, ceramic glass, sandstone, galvanised steel
Photo credits	Simon Wood

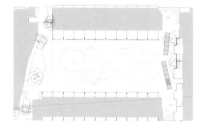

The design of this interior patio marked off by apartment blocks containing 224 apartments, commemorates the 50th anniversary of the discovery of the DNA structure. Form/Lot 302 formally combines the design of a garden courtyard, the possibilities of a communal space and the artwork applied to its landscaping. The elements are arranged in a fluctuating elastic manner and its apparent patchwork pays homage to the genetic code of living organisms and the fluidity of nature. Faithful to their aim, the planners settled on materials with low-environmental impact. The result is a plastic and sculptural creation that culminates in a swimming pool on the upper level, one that resembles a bathtub that incorporates large scale images on its white walls.

Le design de ce patio intérieur, délimitant ces blocs d'appartements pour 224 unités, commémore le 50e anniversaire de la découverte de la structure de l'ADN. Form/Lot 302 est une combinaison formelle alliant le design propre à une toiture avec jardin, les possibilités d'un espace communal et le travail artistique appliqué à l'éthique paysagiste. La disposition des éléments, élastique, fluctuante, ressemblant à un *patchwork*, rend hommage aux processus génétiques des organismes vivants et à la fluidité de la nature. Fidèle à ce but, la conceptrice penche pour des matériaux à faible impact sur l'environnement. Le résultat affiche tout un exercice plastique et sculptural qui, sur la terrasse supérieure, s'achève avec la piscine, qui, telle une baignoire, intègre des illustrations de grand format sur ses murs blancs.

Die Gestaltung dieses Innenhofes, der von Appartementblöcken mit 224 Wohnungen umgeben ist, erinnert an den 50. Jahrestag der Entdeckung der Struktur des ADN. Form/Lot 302 kombiniert die Formen des von ihnen gestalteten, begrünten Dachs, die Möglichkeiten eines gemeinschaftlich genutzten Platzes und das „Kunstwerk", das mit dieser Landschaftsgestaltung geschaffen werden sollte. Die Anordnung der Elemente mit elastischem, fließendem Aussehen und das augenfällige Patchwork stellen die genetischen Prozesse der lebendigen Organismen und das Fließen der Natur dar. Dieser Linie treu, wählten die Planer auch Materialien, die die Umwelt nur wenig beeinflussen. Das Ergebnis ist ein plastisches und skulpturales Gesamtbild, wobei sich auf der oberen Terrasse noch ein Swimmingpool befindet, eine Art Badewanne mit großen Abbildungen an den weißen Wänden.

Il disegno di questo cortile interno, delimitato da blocchi di appartamenti di 244 unità, commemora il 50° anniversario della scoperta della struttura del DNA. Form/Lot 302 combina formalmente il design proprio di una copertura con giardino con le possibilità di uno spazio comune e un *artwork* applicato all'estetica paesaggista. La disposizione degli elementi, elastica e fluttuante, in apparenza dall'aspetto di un *patchwork*, è un omaggio ai processi genetici degli esseri viventi e alla fluidità della natura. A tal fine, il progettista si è risolto per materiali di basso impatto ambientale. Ne risulta un esercizio plastico e scultoreo che culmina — nella terrazza superiore — in una piscina, una sorta di vasca da bagno che accoglie illustrazioni di grandi dimensioni sulle sue pareti bianche.

El diseño de este patio interior, que delimitan estos bloques de apartamentos para 224 unidades, rememora el 50° aniversario del descubrimiento de la estructura del ADN. Form/Lot 302 combina formalmente el diseño propio de una cubierta ajardinada, las posibilidades de un espacio comunal y el *artwork* aplicado a la ética paisajística. La disposición de los elementos, con su aspecto elástico, fluctuante y su aparente *patchwork*, rinde homenaje a los procesos genéticos de los organismos vivos y a la fluidez de la naturaleza. Fiel a dicho propósito, el proyectista se decanta por materiales de bajo impacto ambiental. El resultado es todo un ejercicio plástico y escultural que en la terraza superior se ve culminado por una piscina, a modo de bañera que incorpora ilustraciones de gran tamaño en sus blancas paredes.

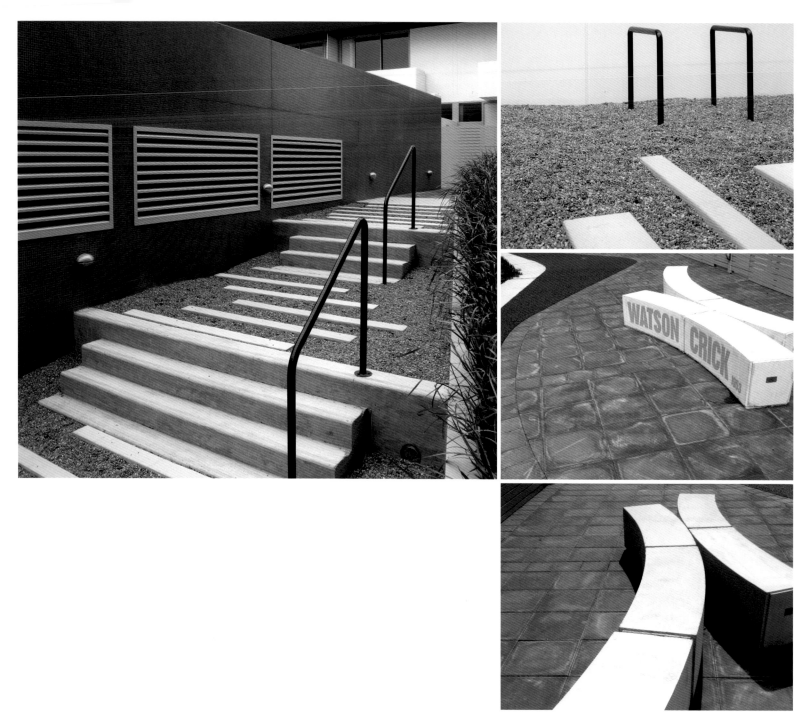

MCGREGOR & PARTNERS | SYDNEY, AUSTRALIA

Website	www.mcgregorpartners.com.au
Project	Former BP Site Public Parkland
Location	Waverton, Sydney, Australia
Year of completion	2005
Materials	concrete, galvanised steel, recycled sandstone, recycled native hardwood timber, decomposed granite
Photo credits	Brett Boardman

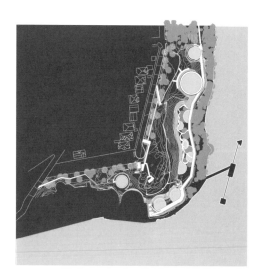

Situated on the Waverton Peninsula, this new public space exists thanks to a political decision: in 1997, local government rejected the residential use of all existing land. Conceived as a dock-side park, the area covers 6 acres upon which, for sixty years, dwelled 31 mineral oil tanks. The new design allowed for some influence from the past, reason for keeping the sandstone embankments made by the old tanks. The result of run-off and infiltration, the water is accumulated in small, newly created ponds. Here it is purified through biological filters comprised of micro-organisms and plants. Among the materials used, concrete and galvanized steel were chosen for their low maintenance and cost.

Situé dans la Péninsule de Waverton, ce nouvel espace public est le fruit d'une décision politique, le gouvernement local ayant refusé, en 1997, l'utilisation résidentielle des terrains existants à cet endroit. Conçu comme un parc portuaire, il occupe 2,5 ha d'une zone qui a hébergé, sept années durant, 31 réservoirs d'huile minérale. Le nouveau design s'inspire du passé, en gardant les terre-pleins en grés qui délimitaient les anciens réservoirs. Fruit de l'érosion et de l'infiltration, l'eau accumulée a formé de nouveaux petits étangs où elle est purifiée grâce à des filtres biologiques, tels les microorganismes et les plantes. Parmi les matériaux utilisés, le béton et l'acier galvanisé ont été sélectionnés pour leur facilité d'entretien et faiblesse de coût.

Dieser neue öffentliche Raum auf der Halbinsel Waverton wurde aufgrund einer politischen Entscheidung geschaffen. Die lokale Verwaltung entschied im Jahr 1997, dass auf den Grundstücken der Halbinsel keine Baugenehmigung für Wohnhäuser erteilt werden sollte. So entstand diese 2,5 ha große Parkanlage am Hafen, in dem in den Sechzigerjahren 31 Mineralöltanks standen. Bei der neuen Gestaltung ließ man sich von der Vergangenheit inspirieren und eliminierte die Aufschüttungen aus Sandstein, die durch die alten Tanks entstanden sind, nicht. Das ablaufende Wasser und Sickerwasser wird in den neu angelegten, kleinen Teichen gestaut, wo es durch biologische Filter aus Mikroorganismen und Pflanzen geklärt wird. Als Materialien wurden Beton und verzinkter Stahl gewählt, da sie preisgünstig sind und kaum pflegebedürftig.

Un nuovo spazio pubblico situato nella penisola di Waverton è frutto di una decisione politica; nel 1997 il governo locale ho dichiarato infatti non edificabile il terreno dove sorge adesso questo parco portuale, che occupa 2,5 ha di una zona utilizzata durante sessanta anni come luogo di stoccaggio per cisterne di olio minerale. Il nuovo disegno tiene conto del passato del luogo e conserva i terrapieni di arenaria che formavano i vecchi depositi. Le acque di deflusso e di infiltrazione sono raccolte in piccole vasche di nuova costruzione, dove sono depurate per mezzo di filtri biologici composti da microrganismi e piante. Per quanto riguarda i materiali, si sono scelti il cemento e l'acciaio galvanizzato a causa del loro basso costo e della facile manutenzione.

Situado en la Península de Waverton, este nuevo espacio público aparece gracias a una decisión política: el gobierno local desestimó, en 1997, el uso residencial de los terrenos allí existentes. Concebido como un parque portuario, ocupa 2,5 ha de una zona que fue, durante sesenta años, morada de 31 tanques de aceite mineral. El nuevo diseño se deja influir por el pasado, por lo que se han conservado los terraplenes de arenisca que dibujaban los antiguos depósitos. Fruto de la escorrentía y la infiltración, el agua es acumulada en pequeños estanques de nueva creación, donde es depurada mediante filtros biológicos formados por microorganismos y plantas. Entre los materiales usados se ha optado por el hormigón y el acero galvanizado, por su bajo mantenimiento y coste.

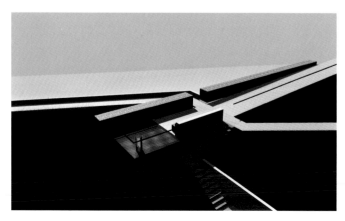

Website	www.oaala.com
Project	Medtronic Corporation Patent Garden
Location	Fridley, Minneapolis, USA
Year of completion	2001
Materials	corten steel, etched stainless steel, riprap, mexican beach pebbles
Photo credits	George Heinrich, Tadd Kreun, Peter Vevang

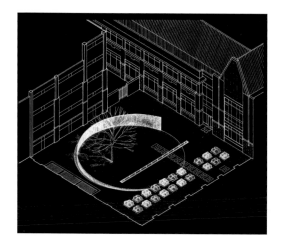

Located on the Medtronic premises, one of the leading firms in the field of biomedical investigation, this is one of the most unique patios among those projected in this scientific compound's master plan. Of Zen inspiration and with pure formal clarity, it lies between a parking lot and a pedestrian path. It was thought to be an area for contemplation, celebration and inspiration that commemorated the over 3,000 patents achieved by the team of scientists and engineers that have worked for the company. The rectangular patio, which is 100 ft. long, boasts surfaces of broken stone. In the center lies a circle planted with grass and semi-closed with 10 ft. high sheets of weathering steel, making this a symbol of the reconciliation between the divine and the human.

Dieser einzigartige Hof, der im Rahmen eines Bebauungsplan für ein Wissenschaftsgelände gestaltet wurde, befindet sich auf dem Firmengelände des Unternehmens Medtronic, einem der Marktführer im Bereich der biomedizinischen Forschung. Der Hof ist deutlich von der Zen-Ästhetik geprägt und zeigt sich in klaren und makellosen Formen. Er liegt zwischen einem Parkplatz und einem Fußgängerweg. Es sollte ein Raum der Betrachtung, der Hommage und der Inspiration entstehen, mit dem man an die über 3 000 Patente erinnert, die die Wissenschaftler und Ingenieure dieses Unternehmens angemeldet haben. Der rechteckige, an den Seiten 30 m lange Hof ist mit zertrümmerten Steinen belegt. Im Zentrum erhebt sich ein mit Rasen bepflanzter, halb mit Stahlblechen aus COR-TEN-Stahl umgebener, 3 m hoher Kreis, ein Symbol für die Versöhnung zwischen dem Göttlichen und dem Menschlichen.

Situado en el campus de la empresa Medtronic, una de las firmas punteras en el campo de la investigación biomédica, éste es uno de los patios más singulares entre los proyectados dentro del master plan para este recinto científico. De inspiración zen y de claridad formal impoluta, se halla entre un aparcamiento y una vía peatonal. Fue pensado como un área de contemplación, celebración e inspiración, que conmemorase las más de 3000 patentes conseguidas por el equipo de científicos e ingenieros que han pasado por dicha empresa. El patio rectangular, de 30 m de lado, presenta superficies de piedra machacada. En el centro se alza un círculo plantado con césped y semicerrado por planchas de acero corten de 3 m de altura, como símbolo de reconciliación entre lo divino y lo humano.

Situé sur le campus de l'entreprise Medtronic, une des entreprises de pointe dans le domaine de la recherche biomédical, ce patio est un des plus originaux parmi ceux conçus dans le master plan de cette enceinte scientifique. D'inspiration zen et d'une pureté formelle immaculée, il se trouve entre un parking et une voie piétonne. Il est conçu comme une zone de contemplation, célébration et inspiration pour commémorer les 3.000 brevets et plus, obtenus par l'équipe de scientifiques et ingénieurs qui ont passé par cette entreprise. Le patio rectangulaire, de 30 m de côté, présente des superficies en pierre broyée. Au centre, s'élève un cercle planté de gazon et à demi clos par des planches d'acier Corten de 3 m de haut, symbole de la réconciliation entre le divin et l'humain.

Situato nel campus dell'azienda Medtronic, una delle firme più importanti nel campo della ricerca biomedica, questo cortile è uno tra i più singolari tra quelli progettati nel quadro del master plan per lo sviluppo di un parco scientifico. Di ispirazione zen e di una tersa nitidezza formale, il cortile è situato tra un parcheggio e un passaggio pedonale e è stato concepito come un'area di contemplazione, celebrazione e ispirazione per commemorare i più di 3000 brevetti ottenuti dal team di scienziati e ingegneri che hanno lavorato per l'azienda. Di forma quadrata e 30 m di lato, presenta superfici in pietra composita. Al centro, un prato circolare, parzialmente chiuso da lastre di acciaio corten alte 3 m, simbolizza la riconciliazione tra divino e umano.

PAOLO L. BÜRGI | CAMORINO, SWITZERLAND

Website	www.burgi.ch
Project	Remembrance Park
Location	Milan, Italy
Renderings	Studio Bürgi

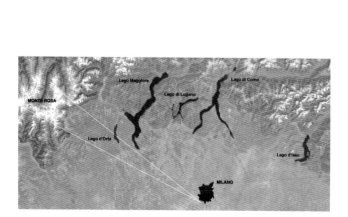

The Swiss landscape architect projected his poetic vision of burial in the outskirts of Milan. In his words, "passage of life" in this space is not conceived as simple cemetery in the traditional sense, but as a place for remembering and for spiritual regeneration. The park is located in a charming valley with a lake in its center. While the graves will be placed on the tree-covered hills around it, the flat area will be left as an open space. The paths are arranged in the shape of a central ring where the rest of the paths begin, becoming the spinal column of a landscape that also plans on having a chapel (*volume* space) and a terrace platform (*void* space), from which one can make out Monte Rosa.

Der Schweizer Landschaftsarchitekt setzte in einem Vorort von Mailand seine poetische Vision einer Grabstätte um. In seinen Worten ist die „Landschaft des Lebens" dieses Raumes nicht wie ein einfacher Friedhof im traditionellen Sinn angelegt, sondern wie ein Ort der Erinnerung und der spirituellen Erneuerung. Der Park liegt in einem freundlichen Tal mit einem See im Zentrum. Die Grabstätten befinden sich auf den umgebenden, bewaldeten Hügeln, während die Ebene als offener Raum erhalten bleibt. Die Wege bilden einen zentralen Ring, von dem die übrigen Pfade abgehen, eine Art Wirbelsäule der Landschaft, in der es auch eine Kapelle und eine terrassenförmige Plattform gibt, von der aus man auf den Monte Rosa blicken kann.

El paisajista suizo proyecta, en las afueras de Milán, su poética visión de la sepultura. En sus palabras, el «paisaje de la vida» de este espacio no es concebido como un simple cementerio en el sentido tradicional, sino como un lugar para el recuerdo y para la regeneración espiritual. El parque se encuentra situado en un gentil valle con un lago en su parte central. Mientras que en los terrenos arbolados de las colinas circundantes se ubicarán los sepulcros, el espacio llano se mantiene como un sitio abierto. La disposición de los viales en forma de anillo central, de donde parten el resto de caminos, conforma la columna vertebral de un paisaje que también planifica una capilla (espacio «volumen») y una plataforma en terraza (espacio «vacío»), desde donde divisar el Monte Rosa.

Le paysagiste suisse projette, dans la banlieue de Milan, sa vision poétique de la sépulture. Comme il l'a dit, le « paysage de la vie » de cet espace n'est pas conçu comme un simple cimetière dans le sens traditionnel, mais comme un lieu de souvenir et de régénération spirituelle. Le parc se situe dans une douce vallée avec un lac au milieu. Les terrains arborés des collines environnantes accueilleront les sépultures et l'espace dans la plaine restera un site ouvert. La disposition des voies en forme d'anneau central, d'où partent les autres chemins, forme la colonne vertébrale d'un paysage qui accueille également une petite chapelle (espace « volume ») et une plateforme en terrasse (espace « vide »), d'où l'on aperçoit le « Monte Rosa ».

L'architetto del paesaggio svizzero ha situato nella periferia di Milano la sua visione poetica della sepoltura. Come lui stesso afferma, il «paesaggio della vita» non è stato concepito come un cimitero tradizionale, ma come uno spazio per il ricordo e la rigenerazione spirituale. Il progetto è situato in una dolce vallata con al centro un lago. Mentre sulle colline alberate circostanti si ubicheranno i sepolcri, il terreno pianeggiante rimarrà uno spazio aperto. La disposizione a forma di anello centrale dei viali, da dove si diramano gli altri sentieri, costituisce la colonna vertebrale di un paesaggio che prevede anche un cappella (spazio/volume) e una piattaforma che funge da terrazza (spazio/vuoto), dalla quale ammirare il Monte Rosa.

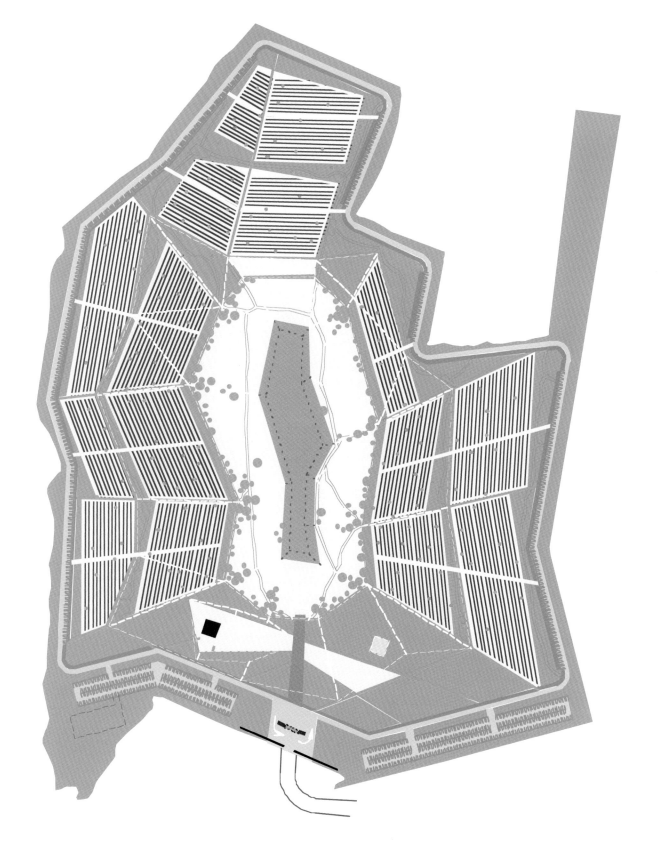

PLOT=BIG+JDS | COPENHAGEN, DENMARK

Website	www.big.dk
Project	Maritime Youth House
Location	Copenhagen, Denmark
Year of completion	2004
Materials	wood, grey concrete, polished aalborg white concrete
Photo credits	Paolo Rosselli, Julien de Smed, Esben Bruun

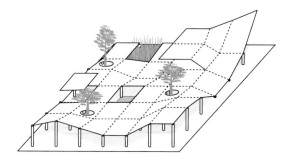

Rather than spend a third of their budget on removing the contaminated grounds of the area, the architects invested in the building's uniqueness, which had to meet two different uses: a sailing club and a youth center. The raised and undulated nature of the wooden roof allows for, on one hand, the boats to moor on the lower part, as well as positioning different halls; on the other hand, it makes it so the youngsters have the entire surface to play on. Unlike other constructions of similar usage, the interior consists of concrete surfaces, while the exterior is covered with wood. The leisure and entertainment aspect of the project explains the importance placed on the activities taking place outdoors.

Statt ein Drittel des Budgets zum Abbau des verseuchten Bodens der Zone auszugeben, investierten die Architekten in ein einzigartiges Gebäude, das verschiedenen Zwecken dient (Segelclub und Jugendzentrum). Am unteren Teil des erhöhten, gewellten Holzdachs können die Boote festgemacht werden. Darunter legte man verschiedene Räume an. Zusätzlich steht das ganze Dach den Jugendlichen zum Spielen zur Verfügung. Im Unterschied zu anderen, ähnlichen Gebäuden sind die ganzen Innenwände mit Beton versehen, während es von außen mit Holz verkleidet ist. Bei diesem Freizeitgebäude wird großer Wert auf die Aktivitäten im Freien gelegt.

En lugar de gastarse un tercio del presupuesto en extraer el suelo contaminado de la zona, los arquitectos invirtieron en la singularidad del edificio, en el que debían converger dos usos diferentes: un club de vela y un centro juvenil. La disposición elevada y ondulada de la cubierta de madera permite, por un lado, el amarre de las embarcaciones en su parte inferior, así como la ubicación de las diferentes salas; por otro, hace que los jóvenes dispongan de toda la cubierta para jugar. A diferencia de otras construcciones de uso similar, los interiores están revestidos con superficies de hormigón, mientras que el exterior está forrado con madera. La componente lúdica y ociosa del proyecto explica la importancia que se atribuye a las actividades realizadas en el exterior.

Au lieu de dépenser un tiers du devis à extraire le sol contaminé de la zone, les architectes ont investi dans l'originalité de l'édifice qui devait réunir deux fonctions distinctes : un club de voile et un centre de jeunes. La disposition en hauteur de la toiture ondulée en bois permet, d'un côté, d'amarrer les embarcations à la partie inférieure, de loger les différentes salles et de l'autre, de laisser aux jeunes disposer de toute la toiture pour jouer. A la différence des autres constructions de ce genre, les intérieurs sont revêtus de béton, alors que l'extérieur est habillé de bois. La composante ludique et de loisir du projet explique l'importance attribuée aux activités réalisées en extérieur.

Invece di spendere un terzo del budget per estrarre il terreno contaminato della zona, gli architetti hanno deciso di investire nella singolarità dell'edificio, che doveva soddisfare due diversi usi: un club nautico e un centro giovanile. La alta copertura ondulata in legno facilita l'attracco delle imbarcazioni e accoglie diverse sale nella sua parte inferiore, mentre la totalità della sua superficie è lasciata disponibile perché i giovani vi possano giocare. A differenza di altre costruzioni simili, i rivestimenti interni sono in cemento, mentre l'esterno è rivestito in legno. Le componente ludica e rilassata del progetto spiega l'importanza attribuita alle attività che si realizzano all'esterno.

RCR ARANDA PIGEM VILALTA ARQUITECTES | OLOT, SPAIN

Website	www.rcrarquitectes.es
Project	Piedra Tosca Park
Location	Les Preses, Spain
Year of completion	2004
Materials	corten steel, volcanic stone
Photo credits	Eugeni Pons

The authors believe "architecture is trees, bushes, vegetation, stones, textures and granulometry". Piedra Tosca Park stretches over 519 acres and its peculiar landscape is a result of the defile of the Croscat Volcano, which erupted 9,500 years B.C. Over time, this place has accumulated volcanic rocks and thick scoria walls, as well as huts and small plots of land for farming. Although it forms part of a natural park, its incipient deterioration required a respectful but determined intervention to preserve its great cultural value. The meticulous reinvention, which reinforces its rough nature while demonstrating their effort to contain the rocks by using open steel slats, make this a unique park that even has space for ecological agriculture.

Die Planer dieses Raums sind der Ansicht, dass „die Architektur die Bäume, Sträucher, Vegetation, Steine, Texturen und Korngrößen sind." Der Bosc de Tosca nimmt eine Fläche von 210 ha ein. Die eigenartige Landschaft ist auf die Aktivitäten des Vulkans Croscat zurückzuführen, der 9 500 Jahre v. Chr. ausgebrochen war. Mit der Zeit haben sich an diesem Ort Vulkangestein und breite Mauern aus Schlacke angesammelt. Ebenso sind Hütten und kleine Felder entstanden. Obwohl der Wald zum Naturpark gehört, machte die beginnende Zerstörung es notwendig, einen vorsichtigen Eingriff durchzuführen, um seinen großen kulturellen Wert zu retten. Die äußerst rücksichtsvolle Neugestaltung, die den rauen Charakter der Landschaft unterstreicht und die stützende Kraft der Felsen durch halboffene Stahlstreifen zeigt, macht diesen Ort zu einem einzigartigen Park, in dem sogar Platz für die ökologische Landwirtschaft ist.

A opinión de sus autores, «la arquitectura son los árboles, arbustos, vegetación, piedras, texturas y granulometrías». El Bosc de Tosca ocupa una superficie de 210 ha y su peculiar paisaje deriva de la colada del volcán Croscat, que hizo erupción 9500 años a.C. Con el tiempo, en este lugar se han acumulado rocas volcánicas y anchos muros de escoria, así como se han instalado barracas y pequeñas parcelas para cultivar. Aunque forma parte de un parque natural, su incipiente deterioro requirió una intervención respetuosa pero decidida para preservar su inmenso valor cultural. La reinvención minuciosa, que refuerza su carácter áspero e ilustra el esfuerzo de contención de las rocas mediante lamas de acero entreabiertas, lo convierte en un parque singular que incluso tiene espacio para la agricultura ecológica.

D'après les auteurs, « l'architecture, ce sont les arbres, arbustes, la végétation, les pierres, les textures granulométries ». Le Bosc de Tosca occupe une superficie de 210 ha et son paysage particulier provient de la coulée de lave du volcan Croscat, dont l'éruption remonte à 9.500 ans av. JC. Au fil du temps, les roches volcaniques et les larges parois de scories se sont accumulées en ce lieu qui accueille des petites baraques et parcelles pour cultiver. Partie intégrante d'un parc naturel, sa détérioration croissante nécessite toutefois une intervention respectueuse de l'environnement, certes, mais déterminée, préservant son immense valeur culturelle. La réinvention minutieuse, renforçant son caractère âpre et illustrant l'effort de retenue des roches, grâce à des lames d'acier entrouvertes, en fait un parc original qui réserve aussi un espace à l'agriculture écologique.

Secondo l'opinione degli stessi autori «l'architettura sono gli alberi, gli arbusti, la vegetazione, le pietre, la texture e la granulometria». Il Bosc de Tosca occupa una superficie di 210 ha e il suo singolare paesaggio è frutto della colata lavica del vulcano Croscat, che eruttò nel 9500 a.C. Col passare del tempo, la zona ha accumulato rocce vulcaniche e ha visto la comparsa di larghi muri fatti di scorie, capanne e piccoli appezzamenti di terreni coltivati, di modo che, sebbene parte di un parco naturale, l'incipiente deterioramento ha richiesto un intervento rispettoso ma deciso per conservarne l'immenso valore culturale. Il minuzioso lavoro di recupero rafforza l'aspro carattere del parco e mette in risalto lo sforzo di contenzione delle rocce mediante lame in acciaio, dando luogo a un progetto singolare che lascia spazio anche all'agricoltura ecologica.

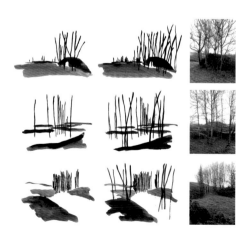

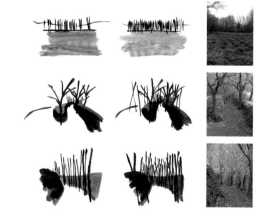

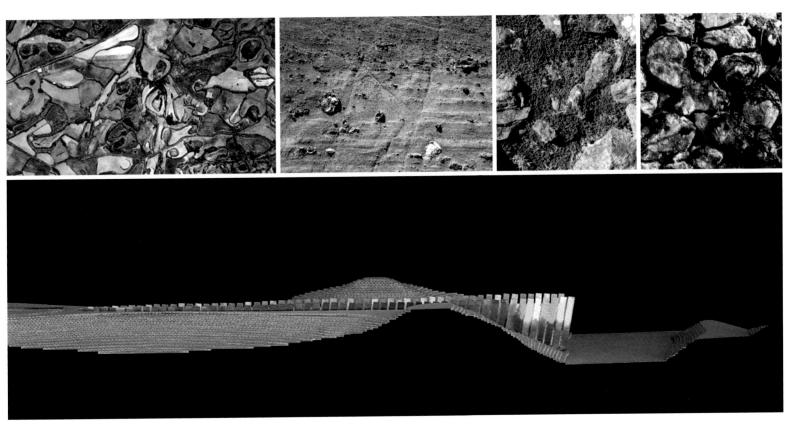

RELAIS LANDSCHAFTSARCHITEKTEN | BERLIN, GERMANY
MOMENTUM3 | HANNOVER, GERMANY

Website	www.relaisLA.de
Project	Schlossplatzareal Berlin
Location	Berlin, Germany
Renderings	relais Landschaftsarchitekten

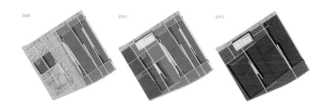

After long political discussion with participation of the citizens, the reconstruction of the old Prussian palace has boiled down to the area which in their day saw the various reincarnations of the Berlin Palace (1701-1973) and the Palace of the Communist Republic (1973-1989; which afterwards had been in disuse until 2005). While its definitive construction has been delayed, in part due to a lack of financing, they are proposing to give this land another use for the meanwhile, a commonplace phenomenon in the German capital. Between constructing and reconstructing, the Berlin studio projects alerce wood walkways elevated 1 ft. over dense greenery, and balustrades above an area of ancient palace ruins. With this fragile and flexible structure they guarantee a quick dismantling, while offering Berliners and tourists a place for recreational use.

Die Rekonstruktion des alten preußischen Palasts wurde nach langen Diskussionen zwischen den Politikern und Bürgern schließlich an dem Ort durchgeführt, an dem sich einst das Berliner Stadtschloss (1701 – 1973) und der Palast der Republik (1973 – 1989) befanden, der dann bis 2005 leer stand. Da es aufgrund fehlender Mittel bis zum endgültigen Bau noch dauern kann, wurde eine Zwischennutzung für das Grundstück gesucht, eine nicht unübliche Lösung in der deutschen Hauptstadt. So entwarf ein Berliner Planungsstudio Holzstege aus Lärchenholz, die sich 30 cm über dem dichten Grün erheben, und Balustraden über den Ruinen des einstigen Schlosses. Diese zerbrechliche und flexible Struktur kann schnell abgebaut werden. Bis zu dieser Demontage dient sie als Freizeitzone für Berliner und Touristen.

La reconstrucción del antiguo palacio prusiano se ha concretado –tras largas discusiones políticas y entre ciudadanos– en el emplazamiento que ocuparon en su momento las diferentes reencarnaciones del Palacio de Berlín (1701-1973) y el Palacio de la República comunista (1973-1989; desde entonces en desuso hasta 2005). Ante la demora de su construcción definitiva, debida en parte a la falta de financiación, se propone un uso intermedio de este solar, fenómeno recurrente en la capital alemana. Entre la construcción y la reconstrucción, el estudio berlinés proyecta pasarelas de madera de alerce, elevadas 30 cm sobre un verde tupido, y balaustradas por encima de una zona de antiguas ruinas del palacio. Con dicha estructura frágil y flexible se asegura un rápido desmontaje y se ofrece una tribuna para el uso recreativo por parte de los berlineses y turistas.

La reconstruction de l'ancien palais prussien se concrétise –après de longues discussions politiques et débats entre citoyens– sur le site occupé, selon les époques, par les différentes réincarnations du Palais de Berlin (1701-1973) et le Palais de la République communiste (1973-1989), depuis lors abandonné jusqu'en 2005. Face au retard de sa reconstruction finale, dû en partie au manque de financement, on a proposé une utilisation temporaire de ce terrain, phénomène récurrent dans la capitale allemande. Entre la construction et la reconstruction, le bureau d'études berlinois projette d'élever des passerelles en cèdre, à 30 cm au-dessus d'une végétation touffue, et des balustrades au-dessus d'une ancienne zone de ruines du palais. Cette structure fragile et flexible, rapidement démontable, offrira, aux berlinois et touristes, une tribune à usage récréatif.

La ricostruzione dell'antico palazzo prussiano si realizzerà – dopo lunghe discussioni politiche e tra i cittadini – nel luogo occupato a suo tempo dalle diverse reincarnazioni del Palazzo di Berlino (1701-1973) e del Palazzo della Repubblica Comunista (1973-1989; in disuso fino al 2005). Visti i ritardi nel completamento dell'opera, dovuti in parte alla mancanza di finanziamenti, si è proposto lo sfruttamento temporaneo del terreno; una soluzione comune nella capitale tedesca. Tra la costruzione e la ricostruzione, lo studio di Berlino ha progettato passerelle in larice – alzate 30 cm al di sopra di un folto prato – e balaustre di fronte a un'area di antiche rovine del palazzo. Tali strutture, fragili e flessibili al tempo stesso, possono essere smontate con facilità e configurano uno spazio ricreativo per gli abitanti e per i turisti.

RUSH WRIGHT ASSOCIATES | MELBOURNE, AUSTRALIA

Website	www.rushwright.com
Project	The Centre for Ideas, Victorian College of the Arts
Location	Southbank, Australia
Year of completion	2004
Materials	black concrete, precast concrete, stainless steel
Photo credits	Peter Bennett

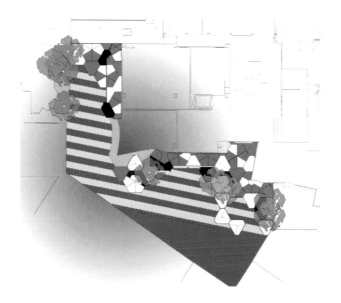

The intervention by this Australian team in the environs of Victoria University's Art School –set between the physical and the digital, the inanimate and the animate– has been defined as pure magic realism. Conceptually speaking, it's an action which confronts an architectural object (the building) with a historically degraded context (the campus). With its intelligent graphic image, its variety of surfaces and its sophisticated geometry based on the figure of a hexagon, at times the landscape takes on a surrealist element and seems inspired on the spatial experiments of Keith Critchlow, author of *Order in Space* (1969). The garden includes indigenous plants that are resistant to the area's microclimate and oak trees originally from River She.

Diesen Eingriff des australischen Studios in der Nähe der Kunstschule des Universitätscampus von Victoria kann man zwischen dem Physischen und dem Digitalen, dem Leblosen und dem Lebenden ansiedeln. Das Ergebnis wurde auch als reiner magischer Realismus definiert. Als grundlegendes Konzept diente die Gegenüberstellung eines architektonischen Objekts (das Gebäude) mit einem im Lauf der Zeit heruntergekommenen Kontext (der Campus). Mit dem auf intelligente Weise gestalteten, grafischen Aussehen, der Verschiedenartigkeit der Flächen und der perfekten Geometrie, die auf dem Sechseck beruht, wirkt der landschaftsarchitektonische Eingriff manchmal fast surrealistisch und scheint von den Raumexperimenten von Keith Critchlow, dem Autoren von „Order in Space" (1969), inspiriert zu sein. Der Garten wurde mit einheimischen Pflanzen angelegt, die dem Mikroklima der Zone widerstehen, und mit Eichen vom She River.

La intervención del equipo australiano en las inmediaciones de la Escuela de Arte del campus universitario de Victoria –situada entre lo físico y lo digital, lo inanimado y lo animado– ha sido definida como puro realismo mágico. Conceptualmente se trata de una acción que confronta un objeto arquitectónico (el edificio) con un contexto históricamente degradado (el campus). Con su inteligente imagen gráfica, su diversidad de superficies y su sofisticación geométrica basada en la figura del hexágono, la acción paisajística por momentos adopta tintes surrealistas y parece inspirada en los experimentos espaciales de Keith Critchlow, autor de *Order in Space* (1969). El ajardinamiento incluye plantas autóctonas, resistentes al microclima de la zona, y robles originarios de River She.

L'intervention de l'équipe australienne aux abords de l'Ecole d'Art du campus universitaire de Victoria –se situant entre le physique et le numérique, l'inanimé et l'animé– se définit comme pur réalisme magique. Sur le plan conceptuel, il s'agit d'une action qui confronte un objet architectural (l'édifice) à un contexte dégradé historiquement (le campus). Fort d'une intelligente image graphique, de sa diversité de surfaces et sa sophistication géométrique basée sur l'hexagone, le paysagisme adopte par moments des nuances surréalistes, semblant s'inspirer des expériences spatiales de Keith Critchlow, autour de *Order in Space* (1969). L'agencement du jardin est composé de plantes autochtones, résistantes au microclimat de la zone, et de chênes rouvres originaires de la « River She ».

L'intervento del team australiano nelle vicinanze della Scuola d'Arte del campus universitario di Victoria si situa tra lo spazio fisico e quello digitale, tra animato e inanimato, e è stato definito come realismo magico allo stato puro. Dal punto di vista concettuale si tratta di un progetto che contrappone un oggetto architettonico (l'edificio) a un contesto storicamente degradato (il campus). Con un'intelligente immagine grafica, una varietà di superfici e una sofisticata geometria basata sulla figura dell'esagono, l'intervento paesaggistico assume toni surrealisti e sembra ispirarsi agli esperimenti spaziali di Keith Critchlow, autore di *Order in Space* (1969). La realizzazione dei giardini comprende piante autoctone, resistenti al microclima della zona, e querce originarie di River She.

R&SIE(N) ARCHITECTS | PARIS, FRANCE

Website	www.new-territories.com
Project	Spidernetthewood
Location	Nimes, France
Year of completion	2007
Materials	polypropylene, steel, wire, concrete, plastic
Photo credits	R&Sie(n) architects

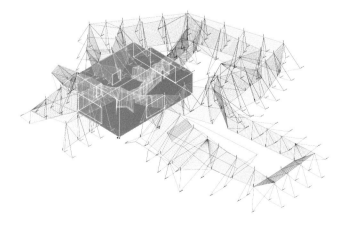

The innovative concept behind this project lies in the creation of a country home entwined like a spider web. In a 1,475 ft^2 building with another 6,560 ft^2 outdoors, they planted a string of trees that will reach their ideal height in five years. The mass of trees is covered by a polypropylene plastic net, creating a labyrinth of sorts between the branches. The actual border between the interior and exterior is blurred by the sensation of porosity and freshness. The areas inside, molded by a denser plastic net are free to be occupied and designed. In a five-year period they hope for the home and exterior netting to melt together with the environment.

Das innovative Konzept dieser Planung besteht in der Schaffung eines Landhauses, das wie ein Spinnennetz verflochten ist. Auf einem Grundstück mit 450 m^2 Wohnfläche und 2000 m^2 Außenbereich wurde eine lange Reihe von Bäumen gepflanzt, die in fünf Jahren ihre Idealhöhe erreichen werden. Die Baumgruppe ist mit einem Kunststoffnetz aus Polypropylen überspannt, so dass eine Art Labyrinth zwischen den Zweigen entsteht. Die wirkliche Grenze zwischen innen und außen wird durch den Eindruck von Porosität und Frische verwischt. Die Räume im Inneren werden von einem weniger durchsichtigem Netz umgeben, und ihre Nutzung und Gestaltung ist noch offen. Man erwartet, dass in fünf Jahren das Haus und das Außennetz ganz mit der Umgebung verschmelzen.

El concepto innovador de este proyecto reside en la creación de una vivienda de campo entrelazada a modo de telaraña. En un solar de 450 m^2 habitables y 2000 m^2 de exterior, se ha plantado una larga ristra de árboles que alcanzarán su tamaño ideal en cinco años. La masa arbolada se recubre con una malla plástica de polipropileno, lo que crea una especie de laberinto entre ramas. La frontera real entre el interior y el exterior queda difuminada por la sensación de porosidad y frescor. Las dependencias del espacio interior, conformadas por una malla plástica más tupida, restan libres para su ocupación y diseño. En el periodo de un lustro se espera que la vivienda y la malla exterior se fundan conjuntamente con el entorno.

Le concept innovant de ce projet réside dans la création d'une habitation de campagne entrecroisée, à l'instar d'une toile d'araignée. Sur un terrain de 450 m^2 habitables et 2.000 m^2 extérieurs, on a planté un long chapelet d'arbres qui atteindront leur taille idéale dans cinq ans. La masse arborée est recouverte d'un filet en plastique de polypropylène, créant ainsi une sorte de labyrinthe entre les branches. La frontière réelle entre l'intérieur et l'extérieur est estompée par la sensation de porosité et de fraîcheur. Les dépendances de l'espace intérieur, configurées par un filet en plastique plus épais, restent libres pour la fonction et le design. D'ici un siècle, l'habitation et le filet extérieur devraient se fondre à l'environnement.

L'idea rivoluzionaria di questo progetto risiede nella concezione di una casa di campagna che si intreccia con la vegetazione come una ragnatela. In un terreno di 2000 m^2, di cui 450 m^2 abitabili, è stata piantata una lunga fila di alberi che raggiungeranno la loro dimensione ideale tra cinque anni. Gli alberi sono stati ricoperti da una rete di polipropilene che crea, assieme ai rami, una specie di labirinto. La frontiera tra interno e esterno si dissolve nella sensazione di porosità e freschezza. Le aree interne, caratterizzate da una rete più fitta, sono state lasciate libere per una posteriore occupazione e un ulteriore disegno. Tra un lustro si prevede che la residenza e la rete esterna si fondano tra loro e con l'ambiente circostante.

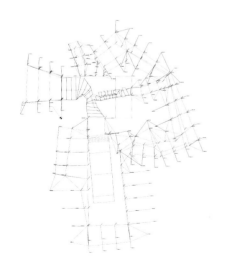

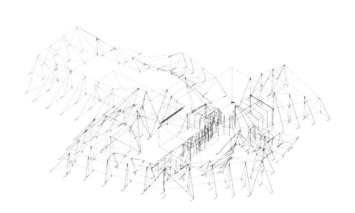

SLA | COPENHAGEN, DENMARK

Website	www.sla.dk
Project	Frederiksberg New Urban Spaces
Location	Frederiksberg, Copenhagen, Denmark
Year of completion	2005
Materials	concrete, golden, iron
Photo credits	Jens Lindhe, Torben Petersen, Lars Bahl

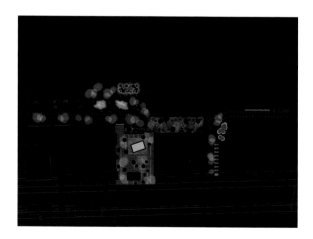

The diagram combines entwined systems, independent sequences and open progressions with the aim of improving the pedestrian walkway and interrelation between passer-bys. In order to create a series of public plazas located between important buildings in Frederiksberg, a city just outside of Copenhagen, the Danish studio SLA opted for a textural solution. The area's climate (cloudy two-thirds of the year) and the presence of water, mark the point of inflection from start to finish. Water is presented in various forms: waterfalls, vapor, rain or still. The result is a chain of spaces animated by the interrelation with this fluid, by the nocturnal lighting, by spectral areas with fog and by the sounds of birds, frogs and owls. The result is an urban experience that, at times, evokes wild nature.

Innerhalb dieses Projekts wurden verknüpfte Systeme, unabhängige Sequenzen und offenes Fortschreiten miteinander kombiniert, um den Durchgang zu ermöglichen und Beziehungen zwischen den Fußgängern entstehen zu lassen. Um eine Reihe öffentlicher Plätze zwischen wichtigen Gebäuden in Frederiksberg, einer Stadt direkt bei Kopenhagen, zu ordnen, hat sich das dänische Studio SLA für eine texturelle Struktur entschieden. Das Klima der Zone (zwei Drittel des Jahres über bewölkt) und das Vorhandensein von Wasser sind der Ausgangspunkt der Planung. Das Wasser erscheint in verschiedenen Formen: als Wasserfall, als Dampf, Regen oder Teich. Das Ergebnis ist eine Reihe von Plätzen, die durch ihre Beziehung zum Wasser, die nächtliche Beleuchtung, die gespenstigen Zonen mit Nebel und den Gesang der Vögel, Frösche und Eulen belebt werden. Eine städtische Erfahrung, die für Momente die wilde Natur heraufbeschwört.

El esquema combina sistemas entrelazados, secuencias independientes y progresiones abiertas, con el fin de potenciar el paso peatonal y la interrelación entre los viandantes. Para el ordenamiento de una serie de plazas públicas, situadas entre edificios importantes de Frederiksberg, ciudad adosada a Copenhague, el estudio danés SLA ha optado por una solución textural. El clima de la zona (nublado dos tercios del año) y la presencia del agua marcan el punto de inflexión de principio a fin. El agua se presenta en formas diversas: cascada, vapor, lluvia o estancada. El resultado es una ristra de espacios animados por la interrelación con ese fluido, por la luminaria nocturna, por zonas espectrales con niebla y por la sonorización de pájaros, ranas y lechuzas. Una experiencia urbana que evoca, por momentos, la naturaleza asilvestrada.

Le schéma conjugue systèmes entrecroisés, séquences indépendantes et progressions ouvertes, afin de valoriser la zone piétonne et la communication entre les voyageurs. Dans l'agencement d'une série de places publiques, situées entre des édifices importants de Frederiksberg, ville adossée à Copenhague, le bureau d'études danois SLA a opté pour une solution texturée. Le climat de la zone (nuageux deux tiers de l'année) et la présence de l'eau marquent le point d'inflexion du début à la fin. L'eau se présente sous diverses formes : cascade, vapeur, pluie ou étangs. Il en résulte un chapelet d'espaces animés de diverses manières : interaction avec ce fluide, éclairage nocturne par zones spectrales avec le brouillard et enfin, bruitage d'oiseaux, grenouilles et de chouettes. Une expérience urbaine qui évoque, par moments, la nature au cœur de la forêt.

Lo schema combina sistemi intrecciati, sequenze indipendenti e progressioni aperte allo scopo di potenziare il passaggio pedonale e la relazione tra i passanti. Per l'intervento su una serie di piazze pubbliche, situate tra importanti edifici di Frederiksberg, una città vicina a Copenaghen, lo studio danese SLA ha optato per una soluzione che dia preminenza alle texture. Le condizioni atmosferiche della zona (il cielo rimane coperto di nuvole per i due terzi dell'anno) e la presenza dell'acqua sono gli elementi fondamentali del progetto. L'acqua si presenta in diverse forme: in cascata, come vapore, pioggia o stagnante. Ne risulta una serie di spazi animati dall'interazione con tale fluido, dall'illuminazione notturna, dalla nebbia che crea zone dall'aspetto spettrale, e dai rumori degli uccelli, le rane e le civette. Uno spazio urbano che evoca continuamente la natura.

SMC ALSOP (SINGAPORE) | SINGAPORE CITY, SINGAPORE

Website	www.smcalsop-sg.com
Project	Clarke Quay Redevelopment
Location	Clarke Quay, Singapore
Year of completion	2006
Materials	steel, ETFE, PTFE, glass reinforced concrete
Photo credits	Jeremy San

The renovation of the Clarke Quay district revolves around revitalizing the 7.4 acre area with a diamond-like shape which had considerably lost its touristic and commercial allure. On one side, the streetscape and the seafront had to become more captivating; on the other, they had to efficiently deal with the extreme weather conditions of the area: heavy rains and high humidity. The alternative to the trite solution of air-conditioning was the creation of a network of arcades throughout the four main streets and central atrium. They achieve a stable temperature (82 °F) thanks to a protective sky made by ETFE (Ethyltetrafluroethylene) suspended from a steel structure. On the seafront they installed platforms lit in different colors which make an allusion to the traditional autumn lantern festivals in this country.

Die Umgestaltung des Viertels Clarke Quay diente der Neubelebung eines 3 ha großen, diamantförmigen Gebietes, das in den letzten Jahren seine touristische und kommerzielle Attraktivität verloren hatte. Einerseits sollten die Straßenlandschaft und die Meerespassage wieder ihre einstige Anziehungskraft erhalten, andererseits musste man effizient die extremen Klimabedingungen der Region bekämpfen, gekennzeichnet von starkem Regen und sehr viel Feuchtigkeit. Die Alternativlösung zu dem abgedroschenen, inneren Durchgang war die Schaffung verflochtener Arkaden entlang der vier Hauptstraßen und des zentralen Atriums. Mit Hilfe eines an einer Stahlstruktur aufgehängten Schutzdachs aus ETFE (Ethyltetrafluoroethylene) wird eine gleichmäßige Temperatur von 28 °C erzielt. An der Meerespassage konstruierte man Plattformen, die in verschiedenen Farben beleuchtet sind. Sie erinnern an die traditionellen Laternen des Herbstfests in diesem Land.

La renovación del distrito de Clarke Quay se sustenta en la revitalización de una zona, de 3 ha y con forma diamantina, que había perdido sustancialmente su atractivo turístico y comercial. Por un lado, el streetscape y el paseo marítimo debían ganar en magnetismo; por otro, se debían combatir eficientemente las extremas condiciones climáticas de la zona: fuerte lluvia y alta humedad. La solución alternativa al manido pasaje interior acondicionado fue la creación de un entramado de arcadas a lo largo de las cuatro calles principales y el atrio central. Se consigue una temperatura estable (28 °C) gracias a un cielo protector formado por ETFE (etiltetrafluoretileno) y suspendido por estructuras de acero. En el paseo marítimo se han instalado plataformas iluminadas con diversos colores, que rememoran los tradicionales faroles del Festival de Otoño de ese país.

La rénovation du district de Clarke Quay repose sur la réhabilitation d'une zone, de 3 ha en forme de diamant, ayant perdu en substance son attrait touristique et commercial. D'un côté, le streetscape (paysage de la rue) et la promenade maritime devait gagner en magnétisme; de l'autre, il fallait combattre efficacement les conditions climatiques extrêmes de la zone : forte pluie et humidité importante. L'alternative à l'ancien passage intérieur, aménagé de manière désuète, affiche un système d'arcades le long des quatre rues principales et un atrium central. Un ciel protecteur constitué de ETFE (Éthyltétrafluoroéthylène) et suspendu par des structures d'acier permet de maintenir une température stable de (28 °C). La promenade maritime est dotée de plateformes éclairées de couleurs diverses, rappelant les réverbères traditionnels du Festival d'Automne de ce pays.

La riabilitazione del distretto di Clarke Quay si concentra sulla rivitalizzazione di una zona a forma di diamante di 3 ha che aveva perso il suo appeal turistico e commerciale. Da una parte, lo streetscape e la passeggiata a mare dovevano guadagnare in magnetismo; dall'altra, era necessario proteggersi dalle estreme condizioni atmosferiche della zona, come le forti piogge e l'elevata umidità. L'alternativa al consueto passaggio interiore climatizzato è stata quella di creare una trama di archi lungo le quattro vie principali e lungo l'atrio centrale. Una copertura in ETFE (etiltetrafluoruroetilene) sospesa da strutture in acciaio mantiene una temperatura stabile di 28 °C. Lungo la passeggiata sono state sistemate piattaforme illuminate con luci di diversi colori, che ricordano i lampioni tradizionali del Festival d'Autunno che si tiene in questo paese.

 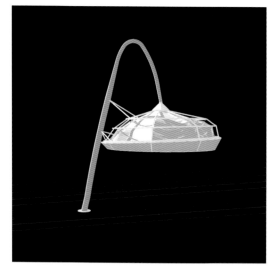

TAYLOR CULLITY LETHLEAN | CARLTON, AUSTRALIA
TONKIN ZULAIKHA GREER | SURRY HILLS, AUSTRALIA

Website	www.tcl.net.au
Project	Craigieburn Bypass
Location	Craigieburn, Australia
Year of completion	2005
Materials	precast concrete, corten steel
Photo credits	Peter Hyatt, John Gollings

The north road of Melbourne becomes a lot more visually attractive with its new design and acoustic screens. It provides a contemporary reading of the place and a design that encourages the ease and fluidity of traditionally static objects. They constructed two types of dividing lines: the Curtain Wall based on a sinuous wall of weathering steel which finishes in a 260 ft. sculptural bridge and connects the Thomastown neighborhood with the Merri Creek Park; and the Scrim wall, closer to the urban center and made of acrylic panels with metallic bands and lighted components, engravings and transparent parts, elements which achieve dynamism according to the driver's rhythm. Its translucent appearance is important for giving off light to the residential area alongside it.

Die Landstraße im Norden von Melbourne ist durch die Neugestaltung und das Aufstellen von Lärmschutzschirmen viel attraktiver geworden. Es handelt sich um eine zeitgenössische Interpretation des Orts und ein Design, das die Hülle und das Fließen von normalerweise eher statischen Objekten verstärkt. Es wurden zwei Arten von Trennlinien angelegt. Die eine ist die Curtain Wall, eine gewellte Mauer aus COR-TEN-Stahl, die zu einer skulpturalen, 80 m hohen Brücke führt, die das Viertel Thomastown mit dem Park Merri Creek verbindet; und die andere die Scrim Wall. Diese liegt näher an der Stadt und besteht aus Akrylpaneelen mit Metallstreifen und Abschnitten mit Licht, Gravuren und transparenten Segmenten, die mit zunehmender Geschwindigkeit dynamischer wirken. Die Lichtdurchlässigkeit ist wichtig, denn so fällt viel Licht in die anliegende Wohnparzelle.

La carretera del norte de Melbourne gana mucho atractivo visual con el nuevo diseño y la implantación de pantallas acústicas. Se trata de una lectura contemporánea del emplazamiento y un diseño que potencia la desenvoltura y fluidez de objetos tradicionalmente estáticos. Se construyeron dos tipos de líneas divisorias: el Curtain Wall, basado en un muro sinuoso de acero corten, que desemboca en un puente escultural de 80 m y enlaza el barrio de Thomastown con el parque de Merri Creek; y el Scrim Wall, más cercano al núcleo urbano y conformado por paneles acrílicos con bandas metálicas y tramas de luces, grabados y segmentos transparentes, elementos que adquieren dinamismo a ritmo del conductor. Su aspecto translúcido es importante para aportar luminosidad a la parcela residencial anexa.

Grâce au nouveau design et à l'installation d'écrans phoniques, la route du nord de Melbourne gagne en intérêt visuel. Il s'agit d'une lecture contemporaine de l'emplacement et d'un design favorisant la légèreté et la fluidité des objets traditionnellement statiques. Le projet a conçu deux lignes de division : d'une part, le Curtain Wall, fondé sur un mur sinueux en acier Corten, qui débouche sur un pont sculptural de 80 m et entoure le quartier de Thomastown avec le parc de Merri Creek. D'autre part, le Scrim Wall, plus proche du centre urbain, est constitué de panneaux acryliques aux bandes métalliques et rames de lumière, de gravures et segments transparents, autant d'éléments qui acquièrent un certain dynamisme au rythme du conducteur. Son aspect translucide est essentiel pour apporter la luminosité nécessaire à la parcelle résidentielle annexe.

La strada del nord di Melbourne guadagna in appeal grazie al nuovo design e ai pannelli fonoassorbenti. Si tratta di una lettura del luogo in chiave contemporanea e di un design che potenzia la disinvoltura e la fluidità di oggetti tradizionalmente statici. Sono stati costruiti due tipi di linee divisorie: il Curtain Wall, un muro sinuoso in acciaio corten, al cui termine si trova un ponte di 80 m di lunghezza che unisce il quartiere del Thomastown con il parco Merri Creek; e lo Scrim Wall, più vicino all'abitato, formato da pannelli acrilici caratterizzati da fasce in metallo e trame luminose, incisioni e zone semitrasparenti, elementi, questi, che acquistano dinamismo al ritmo della guida. L'uso di materiali traslucidi è fondamentale per non sottrarre luminosità alla vicina zona residenziale.

TODD SAUNDERS | BERGEN, NORWAY

Website	www.saunders.no
Project	Solberg Tower
Location	Sarpsborg, Norway
Renderings	Todd Saunders

The building is located right on the border between Sweden and Norway, so that as of 2009, this park will be the first thing one finds upon entering Nordic territory. This project, in cooperation with various municipalities, the regional government and the department of state highways, consists of two elements: weathering steel on the exterior perimeter and wood for the interior elements in a total area of 6,560 ft². The interior is comprised of a park that culminates with a 164 ft. tower, from which one makes out the Oslo fiord. Its spatial distribution creates debate over the intrinsic peculiarities of the place: vertical versus horizontal, slowness versus velocity and contemporary versus the traditional architecture of the area, based on agricultural communities.

Dieser Ort liegt an der Grenzlinie zwischen Schweden und Norwegen, so dass der Park ab 2009 das Erste sein wird, das die Besucher sehen, die mit dem Auto in den Norden fahren. Die Parkanlage entstand in Zusammenarbeit zwischen verschiedenen Gemeinden, der Regionalregierung und der Abteilung für staatliche Autobahnen. Sie besteht aus zwei Elementen, COR-TEN-Stahl an der Außenumfassung und Holz für die inneren Elemente auf einer Fläche von 2 000 m². Im Inneren liegt ein Park mit einem 50 m hohen Turm, von dem aus man auf den Fjord von Oslo blickt. Die Raumaufteilung geht auf die Besonderheiten des Geländes ein. Das Senkrechte wird dem Waagerechten gegenübergestellt, die Langsamkeit der Schnelligkeit und die Moderne der traditionellen regionalen Architektur der ländlichen Gemeinden.

El emplazamiento se sitúa justo en la línea limítrofe entre Suecia y Noruega, de forma que este parque será, a partir de 2009, lo primero que encontrarán los visitantes que entren con coche al territorio nórdico. Este proyecto, en cooperación con diversos municipios, el gobierno regional y el departamento de autopistas estatales, consta de dos elementos: acero corten en el perímetro exterior y madera para los elementos del interior, en un área total de 2000 m². El interior está conformado por un parque que culmina con una torre de 50 m, desde donde se divisa el fiordo de Oslo. La distribución espacial plantea debates sobre las peculiaridades intrínsecas del sitio: lo vertical versus lo horizontal, la lentitud versus la celeridad y lo contemporáneo versus la arquitectura de la zona, basada en comunidades agrícolas.

Le site se trouvant juste aux confins de la Suède et de la Norvège, fait que ce parc sera, à partir de 2009, le premier que rencontreront les visiteurs pénétrant en en voiture sur le territoire nordique. Ce projet, réalisé en commun avec diverses municipalités, le gouvernement régional et le département d'autoroutes publiques, affiche deux matériaux : l'acier Corten pour le périmètre extérieur et le bois pour les éléments de l'intérieur, sur une surface totale de 2.000 m². L'intérieur est configuré comme un parc dont le point culminant est une tour de 50 m, d'où l'on aperçoit le fiord d'Oslo. La distribution spatiale affiche le débat sur les particularités inhérentes au site : le vertical versus l'horizontal, la lenteur versus la vitesse et le contemporain versus l'architecture de la zone, constituée de communautés agricoles.

Il sito si trova esattamente sulla linea di confine tra Svezia e Norvegia, di modo che, a partire dal 2009, questo parco sarà la prima cosa che vedranno i viaggiatori che attraverseranno la frontiera in macchina. Nel progetto — frutto della cooperazione tra vari municipi, il governo regionale e la società delle autostrade statali — si possono individuare due materiali: l'acciaio corten, usato nel perimetro esterno, e il legno, utilizzato per gli elementi situati all'interno, in un'area totale di 2000 m². All'interno vi è un parco in cui spicca una torre alta 50 m, dalla cima della quale si può scorgere il fiordo di Oslo. La distribuzione spaziale dei diversi elementi ha suscitato un dibattito sulle caratteristiche spesso contrapposte del sito: verticale e orizzontale, lento e veloce, design contemporaneo e architettura tradizionale della zona, fondata su comunità agricole.

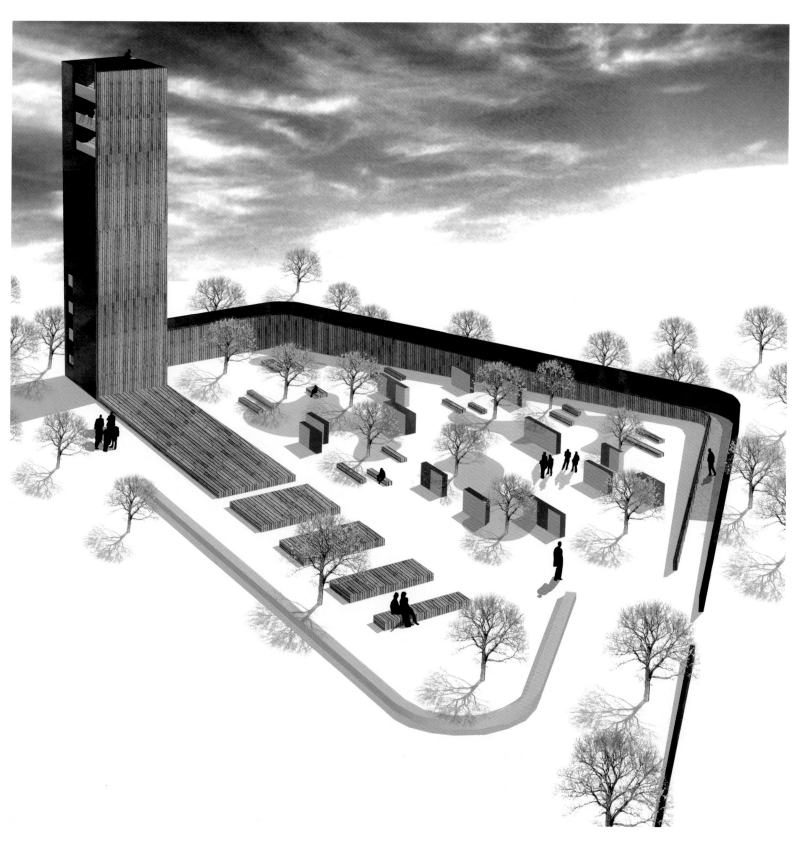

TODD SAUNDERS | BERGEN, NORWAY
TOMMIE WILHELMSEN | STAVANGER, NORWAY

Websites	www.saunders.no	www.tommie-wilhelmsen.no
Project	Aurland Lookout
Location	Aurland, Norway
Year of completion	2006
Materials	steel, laminated wood, glass
Photo credits	Todd Saunders

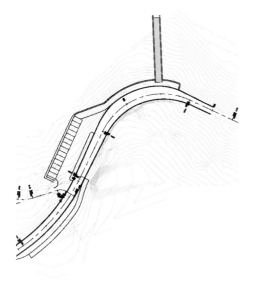

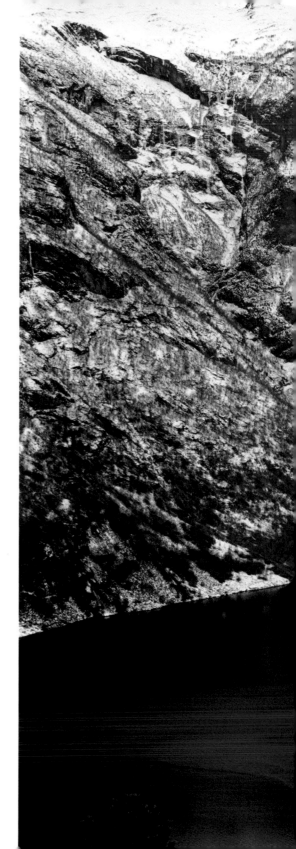

Located three hours from Bergen, on the west coast of Norway, Aurland is an obligatory stop for the tourist sector due to its impressive views of the Sogn of Fjordane fiord. Human pressure in the enclave justified a landscape solution that, on one side, ought to respect the surroundings (favorable visual impact and caution with the pine trees in the area) and, on the other, allow for tourism to enjoy nature in the most direct way possible. The Canadian-Norwegian duo opted to build a fragile pine wood structure 100 ft. away from the highest point of the fiord and suspended from a steel structure anchored into a concrete base. The project invites visitors to cross the walkway, located almost 2,000 ft. above ground, until reaching the other end, where the only thing beneath their feet is a sheet of tempered glass.

Aurland, drei Stunden von den Bergen an der Westküste Norwegens entfernt gelegen, ist ein Ort, an dem die Touristen stets halt machen, um den beindruckenden Blick auf den Fjord Sogn og Fjordane zu genießen. Aufgrund des Besucherzustroms musste eine landschaftliche Lösung gesucht werden, die zum einen die Natur respektiert, d. h. sich gut in die Landschaft einpasst und die Kiefern der Region nicht schädigt, und die es zum anderen dem Touristen möglich macht, die Natur so direkt wie möglich zu genießen. Das kanadisch-norwegische Planerduo wählte eine zerbrechlich wirkende Struktur aus Kiefernholz, die 30 Meter vom höchsten Punkt des Fjords entfernt und an einer Stahlstruktur aufgehängt ist, die wiederum in einer Betonbasis verankert ist. Der Besucher kann über diesen 600 m über dem Boden schwebenden Laufsteg bis ans Ende gehen, wo ihn nur eine Platte aus gehärtetem Glas von dem Abgrund trennt.

Situado a tres horas de Bergen, en la costa oeste de Noruega, Aurland es una parada obligatoria del sector turístico, por las imponentes vistas del fiordo Sogn of Fjordane. La presión humana en el enclave justificaba una solución paisajística que, por un lado, respetase el entorno (impacto visual favorable y precaución con los pinos de la zona) y, por otro, permitiese al turismo disfrutar de la naturaleza de la forma más directa posible. El dúo canadiense-noruego optó por levantar una frágil estructura de madera de pino, a 30 m del punto más alto del fiordo y suspendida por una estructura de acero anclada en una base de hormigón. El proyecto invita al visitante a recorrer la pasarela, situada a 600 m del suelo, y acceder a su extremo, únicamente separado del vacío por una placa de cristal temperado.

Situé à trois heures de Bergen, sur la côte ouest de Norvège, Aurland est un arrêt touristique obligatoire, pour les vues imposantes sur le fiord « Sogn of Fjordane ». La densité humaine dans l'enclave justifiait une solution paysagée qui, d'un côté, doit respecter l'environnement (impact visuel favorable et protection des pins de la zone) et de l'autre, permettre aux touristes de jouir de la nature le plus directement possible. Le duo canado-norvégien a choisi d'élever une structure fragile en bois de pin, à 30 m du point le plus élevé du fiord, suspendue par une structure d'acier ancrée sur un socle de béton. Le projet invite le visiteur à parcourir la passerelle, située à 600 m du sol, et d'accéder à l'extrémité, juste séparé du vide par une plaque de verre trempé.

Situato a tre ore da Bergen, sulla costa ovest della Norvegia, Aurland è una fermata obbligatoria per i turisti grazie alle spettacolari viste che da lì si godono del fiordo Sogn og Fjordane. L'elevato afflusso di visitatori giustificava una soluzione di architettura del paesaggio che, da una parte, rispettasse l'ambiente – riducendo al minimo l'impatto visuale e usando speciale cautela con i pini della zona –, dall'altra, permettesse ai turisti di stare il più possibile a contatto con la natura. Il duo di architetti canadese e norvegese ha progettato una fragile struttura in legno di pino, situata a 30 m dal punto più alto del fiordo e sospesa a una struttura in acciaio ancorata a una base di cemento. Il visitatore è invitato a percorrere la passerella – situata a 600 m dal suolo – fino alla sua estremità, dove una unica lastra di vetro temperato lo separa dal vuoto.

TURENSCAPE | BEIJING, CHINA

Website	www.turenscape.com
Project	The Red Ribbon/Tanghe River Park
Location	Qinhuangdao City, Hebei Province, China
Year of completion	2006
Materials	fibreglass, steel
Photo credits	Kongjian Yu, Cao Yang

Located on the banks of the Tanghe River at the height of the city of Quinhuangdao, Red Ribbon extends throughout 1,640 ft. with a width that varies between 1 and 5 feet. It serves as a bench, walkway, light source (thanks to its red interior lights) and a vantage point. The sinuous red ribbon is only interrupted by four pavilions which protect one from the climate or serve as meeting points. The area, currently covered by dense vegetation and a potential nest for various bird species, used to be a landfill site with old hydrological infrastructures (irrigation ditches, water towers) used to farm these lands. With the new design, this old marginal area has improved in its recreational aspects (fishing, swimming, jogging).

Das Red Ribbon (rotes Band) erstreckt sich über eine Strecke von 500 m mit einer Breite zwischen 30 bis 150 cm am Ufer des Flusses Tanghe bei der Stadt Quinhuangdao entlang. Es dient als Bank, Laufsteg, Lichtquelle mit rötlichen Beleuchtungskörpern und als Aussichtsterrasse. Das kurvige, rote Band wird nur von vier Pavillons unterbrochen, die vor dem Wetter schützen und als Treffpunkt dienen. Die Zone, in der sich heute eine üppige Vegetation und Nistplätze für viele Vogelarten befinden, war einst eine Mülldeponie mit alten hydrologischen Anlagen (Bewässerungsgraben, Wasserturm), die dem Bewässern des Landes dienten. Durch die Neugestaltung hat dieses einstige Randgebiet an Reiz für die Freizeitgestaltung gewonnen (Fischfang, Schwimmen, Jogging).

Situado en la ribera del río Tanghe, a la altura de la ciudad de Quinhuangdao, el Red Ribbon (lazo rojo) se extiende a lo largo de 500 m y con un ancho variable de 30-150 cm. Cumple las funciones de banco, pasarela, foco de iluminación (gracias a las luces interiores, de tono rojizo) y atalaya. La sinuosa banda roja sólo es fragmentada por cuatro pabellones, que protegen del clima o sirven como punto de encuentro. El área, recubierta actualmente por una extensa vegetación y nido potencial de diversas especies de aves, era antes un vertedero con antiguas infraestructuras hidrológicas (acequias, torres de agua) usadas para conrear esas tierras. Con el nuevo diseño, esta antigua zona marginal ha potenciado su lado recreativo (pesca, natación, *jogging*).

Situé sur la rive du fleuve Tanghe, à la hauteur de la ville de Quinhuangdao, le Red Ribbon (ruban rouge) s'étend sur une longueur de 500 m et sur une largeur variable de 30-150 cm. Il est à la fois banc, passerelle, foyer d'éclairage (par le biais de lumières intérieures, rougeâtres) et de tour de guet. La bande rouge sinueuse n'est interrompue que par quatre pavillons qui protègent contre le climat ou servent de point de rencontre. La zone, actuellement recouverte d'une abondante végétation, nid potentiel de diverses espèces d'oiseaux est une ancienne décharge aux infrastructures hydrologiques désuètes (canal d'irrigation châteaux d'eau) utilisées pour cultiver ces terres. Grâce au nouveau design, cette ancienne zone marginale exalte l'aspect récréatif (pêche, natation, *jogging*).

Situato sulla sponda del fiume Tanghe, all'altezza della città di Quinhuangdao, il Red Ribbon (fiocco rosso) si snoda per 500 m, con una larghezza variabile tra i 30 e i 150 cm, svolgendo la funzione di panchina, passerella, punto di illuminazione — grazie alle luci interne dal tono rossastro — e di belvedere. La sinuosa striscia rossa è interrotta solamente da quattro padiglioni, che servono per proteggersi dalle intemperie e come punto di incontro. L'area, ricoperta attualmente da una folta vegetazione e potenziale luogo di nidificazione per diverse specie di uccelli, era in precedenza una discarica con resti di una vecchia struttura (canali, cisterne) usata per irrigare i terreni circostanti. Grazie a questo progetto, è stato possibile recuperare una zona in precedenza degradata, dove adesso si possono svolgere attività come la pesca, il nuoto o il *jogging*.

URBANUS | SHENZHEN, CHINA

Website	www.urbanus.com.cn
Project	Diwang Park B
Location	Shenzhen, China
Year of completion	2005
Materials	concrete, steel, glass
Photo credits	Yan Meng, Jiu Chen

Occupying an area of 13,120 ft², the park is located in an intersection of busy avenues in Shenzhen, below which flows a subterranean channel. The Diwang building, the city's tallest, gives it its name and is raised beside this park with such a heavy urban accent: undulating lines, lights and colors as a reflection of a changing, energetic city. Its design aims to unite the irregularity and discontinuity of its surroundings. The presence of bamboo, boxed in glass cubes, serves as a lit point and as a counterpoint to this urban enclave's dynamism. In the central part, there's a bathroom with a black metal structure that is discordant with the rest of the complex.

Dieser 4 000 m² große Park liegt an de Kreuzung zweier belebter Boulevards von Shenzhen. Unter der Fläche fließt ein unterirdischer Kanal. Das Gebäude Diwang, das höchste der Stadt, gibt ihm seinen Namen. Es steht im Osten dieser betont städtischen Parkanlage mit gewellten Linien, Lichtern und Farben, die die energische, sich verändernde Stadt widerzuspiegeln scheinen. Mit der Gestaltung der Anlage sollten auch die Unregelmäßigkeit und die fehlende Verbindung in der Umgebung ausgeglichen werden. Bambus in Glaswürfeln dient als Beleuchtungskörper und ruhiger Kontrapunkt zu der Hektik der umgebenden Stadt. Im Zentrum verstärkt eine mit einer schwarzen Metallstruktur verkleidete Toilette die Diskordanz der Umgebung.

Ocupando una superficie de 4000 m², el parque está situado en una intersección de las concurridas avenidas de Shenzhen, debajo de cuya superficie circula un canal subterráneo. El edificio Diwang, el más alto de la ciudad, da nombre y se levanta al lado de este parque con marcado acento urbano: líneas onduladas, luces y colores, como reflejo de una ciudad cambiante y energética. Su diseño persigue también unificar la irregularidad y discontinuidad del entorno. La presencia del bamboo, encajonado en cubos de cristal, sirve de punto iluminado y de contrapunto al dinamismo propio de este enclave urbano. En la parte central, un lavabo revestido con una estructura metálica negra marca la discordancia con el conjunto.

Avec une superficie de 4.000 m², le parc est situé à l'intersection des avenues fréquentées de Shenzhen, sous lequel coule un canal souterrain. L'édifice Diwang, le plus haut de la ville, et son image de marque, s'élève à côté de ce parc à fort caractère urbain : lignes ondulées, lumières et couleurs, reflets d'une ville changeante et dynamique. Son design tente d'unifier l'irrégularité et la discontinuité de l'environnement. La présence du bambou, encaissé dans des cubes de verre, sert de point d'éclairage et de contrepoint au dynamisme propre à cette enclave urbaine. Dans la partie centrale, un lavabo revêtu d'une structure métallique noire se démarque du reste.

Il parco, con una superficie di 4000 m², è situato all'incrocio di due trafficate strade di Shenzhen, al di sotto delle quali scorre un canale sotterraneo. L'edificio Diwang, il più alto della città, sorge accanto a questo omonimo parco dal carattere decisamente urbano, dove linee sinuose, luci e colori sono il riflesso di una città piena di energia e in costante evoluzione. Il disegno cerca di unificare un'area irregolare e discontinua. Il bambù, collocato in cubi di vetro, fa, al tempo stesso, da punto luce e da contrappunto al dinamismo che caratterizza questo area urbana. Al centro, un lavabo rivestito da una struttura metallica di colore nero è la nota dissonante del complesso.

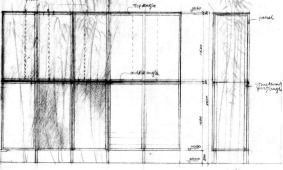

337

URBANUS | SHENZHEN, CHINA

Website	www.urbanus.com.cn
Project	Sungang Central Plaza
Location	Shenzhen, China
Year of completion	2006
Materials	concrete, steel, glass
Photo credits	Yan Meng, Jiu Chen

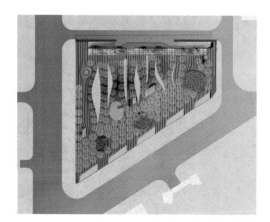

Dynamism governs the design of this urban space. The initial project contemplated a 32,800 ft² two-floor subterranean parking, a subterranean plaza and a green belt on its southern side. At the last minute the client ordered them to reconsider the proposal presented for the surface top. Urbanus thought to reactivate the plaza using curved geometry full of bends and turns. Inspired on the natural texture of earth, the surface is covered with a layer of undulated strips that recall the movement of the tides. In addition to serving as a cover, this sheath serves as a nexus between the two adjacent parking lots. The mosaic created by the strips is only interrupted by small islands of flowers, creating a visual effect that diminishes the impact of its bustling surroundings.

Die Gestaltung dieser städtischen Anlage ist von einer gewissen Dynamik geprägt. Zunächst sollte ein unterirdisches, zweistöckiges Parkhaus auf 10 000 m² Fläche entstehen, ein ebenfalls unterirdischer Platz und ein Grünstreifen an der Südflanke. Der Auftraggeber änderte im letzten Augenblick seine Pläne und gab auch die Gestaltung des oberirdischen Teils in Auftrag. Urbanus gestaltete den Platz mit einer kurvigen Geometrie voller Biegungen. Von der natürlichen Textur der Erde inspiriert, ist die Oberfläche wie von einer Haut aus gewellten Streifen überzogen, die an die Bewegung der Gezeiten erinnert. Diese Haut dient nicht nur als Dach, sondern sie bildet auch die Verbindung zwischen zwei anliegenden Parkplätzen. Das Mosaik, das durch die Streifen geschaffen wird, wird nur von kleinen Blumeninseln unterbrochen, ein visueller Effekt, der die Umgebung ruhiger wirken lässt.

El dinamismo rige el diseño de este espacio urbano. El proyecto inicial contemplaba un aparcamiento subterráneo de dos pisos y 10.000 m², una plaza también subterránea y un cinturón verde por el flanco sur. El cliente ordenó, a última hora, reformular la propuesta presentada para la capa de la superficie. Urbanus apuesta por reactivar la plaza mediante una geometría curvada y llena de recodos. Inspirados por la textura natural de la tierra, la superficie se reviste con una piel a bandas onduladas, que recuerda el movimiento de las mareas. Esta piel, aparte de servir de cobertizo, también funciona como nexo entre dos aparcamientos adyacentes. El mosaico generado por las bandas se ve sólo interrumpido por pequeñas islas de flores, en un efecto visual que aminora el ajetreo circundante.

Le dynamisme régit le design de cet espace urbain. Le projet initial envisageait la construction d'un *parking* souterrain de deux étages sur 10.000 m², une place également souterraine et une ceinture verte sur le flanc sud. Le client, à la dernière minute, a demandé de changer la proposition présentée pour la couche de la superficie. Urbanus mise sur la réactivation de la place par le biais d'une géométrie toute en courbes, remplie de méandres. Imitant la texture naturelle de la terre, la superficie est recouverte d'une membrane à bandes ondulées, rappelant le mouvement des marées. Cette enveloppe, hormis sa fonction d'auvent, sert également de lien entre deux appartements adjacents. La mosaïque générée par les bandes n'est interrompue que par de petites îles de fleurs, créant un effet visuel qui minimise l'agitation environnante.

Il dinamismo è alla base del disegno di questo spazio urbano. Il progetto iniziale prevedeva un parcheggio sotterraneo a due piani di 10000 m², una piazza, anch'essa sotterranea e una zona verde nel lato sud. All'ultimo momento, il cliente ha chiesto di riformulare la proposta per la parte in superficie. Urbanus ha deciso di rinnovare la piazza attraverso una geometria curva ricca di pieghe. Traendo ispirazione dalla texture naturale della terra, la superficie è stata rivestita con una pelle a strisce sinuose che ricordano il movimento delle maree e che, oltre a fare da copertura, funziona da nesso tra i due parcheggi adiacenti. Il mosaico formato dalle strisce è interrotto da piccole aiole di fiori, che creano un effetto visuale che contribuisce a smorzare il trambusto della zona.

VERZONE WOODS ARCHITECTES | ROUGEMONT, SWITZERLAND

Website	www.vwa.ch
Project	Las Margas Parks and Gardens
Location	Latas, Spain
Year of completion	2008 (1st stage)
Materials	prefabricated concrete, coloured concrete, local stone, wood, corten steel, water, glass, steel
Photo credits	Verzone Woods Architectes/Craig Verzone, Nozar SA

With an ambitious program of 2,200 inhabitable apartments, 27 golf holes, a clubhouse, a hotel, commercial areas, schools, social centers, public parks, private gardens and almost 200 acres of natural reserve, the plan for Margas is underway in the tiny municipality of Latas at the foot of the Pyrenees. The program, developed between 2004 and 2015, will increase the population by 9,000. Located in an old agricultural area that is currently barren, the complex's green lung converges around a main pedestrian walkway and five artificial water reserves (for watering the gardens and golf course), which are interrelated and flanked by paths, stairs and ramps. The intersection between vertical pedestrian steps and the main transversal walkway is resolved by creating squares.

Im Rahmen dieses ehrgeizigen Projektes entstanden 2 200 Wohneinheiten, 27 Golflöcher, ein Clubhaus, ein Hotel, Gewerberäume, Schulen, Sozialzentren, öffentliche Parkanlagen, private Gärten und etwa 80 ha Naturschutzgebiet. Diese Anlage von Las Margas befindet sich in der kleinen Gemeinde Latas am Fuße der Pyrenäen. Die Bebauung findet zwischen 2004 und 2015 statt. Die Bevölkerungszahl wird sich dadurch um 9 000 Personen erhöhen. Das Gelände liegt in einem ehemaligen Landwirtschaftsgebiet, heute unfruchtbar, und die grüne Lunge des Gebäudekomplexes erstreckt sich entlang der Hauptpromenade und vorbei an fünf künstlichen Wasserteichen, die dem Bewässern der Gärten und des Golfplatzes dienen. Sie sind miteinander verbunden und von Wegen, Treppen und Rampen umgeben. Die Kreuzungen zwischen den senkrecht verlaufenden Fußgängerwegen und der quer verlaufenden Hauptpromenade sind in Form von Plätzen angelegt.

Con un ambicioso programa de 2200 unidades habitables, 27 hoyos de golf, un clubhouse, un hotel, espacios comerciales, escuelas, centros sociales, parques públicos, jardines privados y cerca de 80 ha de reserva natural, el plan para las Margas se levanta en el pequeño municipio de Latas, a los pies del Pirineo. El programa, en desarrollo entre 2004 y 2015, representará un aumento demográfico de 9000 personas.Situado en una antigua zona agrícola actualmente infértil, el pulmón verde del complejo converge y se articula en torno a un paseo principal y cinco reservas de agua artificiales (para riego de jardines y el campo de golf), interrelacionadas entre sí y flanqueadas por caminos, escaleras y rampas. La intersección entre pasos peatonales verticales y el paseo principal en forma transversal se resuelve mediante la abertura de plazas.

2.200 unités habitables, 27 trous de golf, clubhouse, hôtel, espaces commerciaux, écoles, centres sociaux, parcs publics, jardins privés et près de 80 ha de réserve naturelle : ce programme ambitieux du projet des Margas s'érige dans la petite commune de Latas, au pied des Pyrénées. Développé entre 2004 et 2015, il représentera une croissance démographique de 9.000 personnes. Situé dans une ancienne zone agricole, devenue infertile, le poumon vert du complexe converge et s'articule au tour d'une promenade principale et cinq réserves d'eau artificielles (pour l'arrosage des jardins et du cour de golf), communiquant entre elles et flanquées de chemins, escaliers et rampes. Des places s'ouvrent à l'intersection des passages piétons verticaux et de la promenade principale de forme transversale.

Il progetto delle Margas, situato nel piccolo municipio di Latas, ai piedi dei Pirenei, ha un ambizioso programma di 2200 unità abitabili, un campo da golf con 27 buche, una clubhouse, un hotel, spazi commerciali, scuole, centri sociali, parchi pubblici, giardini privati e circa 80 ha di parco naturale. L'intervento, iniziato nel 2004 e da terminare nel 2015, determinerà un incremento demografico nella zona di 9000 persone. Situato in una zona agricola attualmente improduttiva, il polmone verde del progetto è articolato intorno a un viale principale e cinque riserve artificiali d'acqua per i giardini e il campo da golf, variamente connesse e fiancheggiate da sentieri, scale e rampe. Delle piazze occupano gli incroci tra il viale principale e i passaggi pedonali ad esso perpendicolari.

VETSCH NIPKOW PARTNER
LANDSCHAFTSARCHITEKTUR BSLA/SIA | ZURICH, SWITZERLAND

Website	www.vnp.ch
Project	Sulzer Areal
Location	Winterthur, Switzerland
Year of completion	2004
Materials	hot-galvanised steel, asphalt sprinkled with steel powder, concrete, gravel, untreated steel, crude steel, plastic
Photo credits	Ralph Feiner

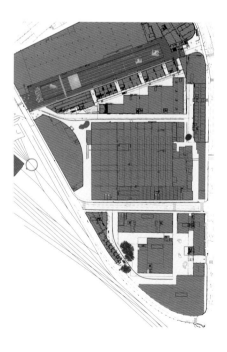

Faithful to the claim "freedom of action is necessary and spaces should be filled with new stories while respecting the esthetics of the past", the architects avoided demolition to give this building a second life. This Winterthur neighborhood is one of the most important post-industrial enclaves of this Alpine country, and has been reconverted in a new 32,800 ft^2 urban space. Here the esthetics of the past (the bays where they used to build diesel motors and turbines) are integrated with the new architecture (modern residences, commercial areas, professional studios and centers); they also make the most of the diaphanous spaces between the buildings to add metal furniture elements, concrete paving, water, colorful lighting and vegetal species that give it a more recreational disposition.

Die Architekten folgten dem Leitsatz: „Die Handlungsfreiheit ist notwendig, die Räume müssen mit neuen Geschichten gefüllt werden, und gleichzeitig muss man die Ästhetik der Vergangenheit respektieren". Deshalb vermieden sie einen Abriss und entschlossen sich dazu, diesem Ort ein zweites Leben zu schenken. Dieses Viertel in Winterthur ist einer der wichtigsten postindustriellen Orte des Alpenlandes. Er wurde zu einem 10 000 m^2 großen, städtischen Raum umgestaltet. Die Ästhetik der Vergangenheit – einst standen hier Werkshallen, in denen Dieselmotoren und Turbinen hergestellt wurden – wurde mit der neuen Architektur verbunden (moderne Wohnhäuser, Geschäfts-zonen, Ateliers und Studios). Auch die Übergangszonen zwischen den Gebäuden wurden mit städtischem Mobiliar aus Metall, Betonböden, Wasser, bunter Beleuchtung und Grünflächen ausgestattet, die eine Freizeitzone entstehen lassen.

Fiel al postulado «la libertad de acción es necesaria y los espacios deben ser rellenados con nuevas historias mientras se respete la estética del pasado», los arquitectos han evitado la demolición para darle una segunda vida al emplazamiento. Este barrio de Winterthur representa uno de los enclaves postindustriales más importantes del país alpino, reconvertido en un nuevo espacio urbano de 10.000 m^2. En éste se integra la estética del pasado (las naves donde anterior-mente se construían motores diesel y turbinas) con la nueva arquitectura (residencias de corte moderno, zonas comerciales, estudios y centros profesionales); también se aprovechan los espacios diáfanos entre edificio y edificio para incorporar elementos de mobiliario de metal, pavimento de hormigón, agua, iluminación de color y especies vegetales que potencian la vocación recreativa.

Fidèle au postulat « la liberté d'action est nécessaire et les espaces doivent être remplis de nouvelles histoires, tout en respectant l'esthé-tique du passé », les architectes ont évité de démolir pour donner une seconde vie au site. Ce quartier de Winterthur représente une des enclaves post-industrielles majeures du pays alpin, reconvertie en un nouvel espace urbain de 10.000 m^2. Sa conception intègre l'esthéti-que du passé (les nefs, anciens lieux de construction des moteurs diesel et des turbines) à la nouvelle architecture (résidences moder-nes, zones commerciales, bureaux d'études et centres profession-nels). Les espaces diaphanes entre les édifices sont optimisés grâce à l'apport d'éléments divers : mobilier en métal, revêtement en béton, eau, éclairage en couleur et espèces végétales qui favorisent la voca-tion récréative de l'ensemble.

Fedeli alla massima «la libertà d'azione è necessaria e gli spazi devono essere riempiti con nuove storie, sempre che si rispetti l'este-tica del passato», gli architetti hanno scongiurato la completa demo-lizione del sito per dargli nuova vita. Questo quartiere di Winterthur, una delle aree postindustriali più importanti del paese alpino, è stato convertito in un nuovo spazio urbano di 10000 m^2, dove l'estetica del passato (i capannoni dove si costruivano motori diesel e turbine) si fonde con la nuova architettura (residenze moderne, zone commer-ciali, studi e centri professionali). Gli spazi liberi tra gli edifici sono occupati da arredi urbani in metallo, da pavimentazione in cemento, dall'acqua, dall'illuminazione colorata e da piante che sottolineano la dedizione del luogo allo svago.

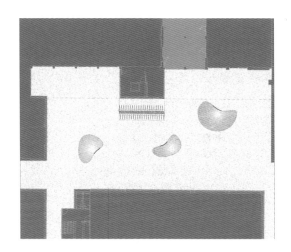
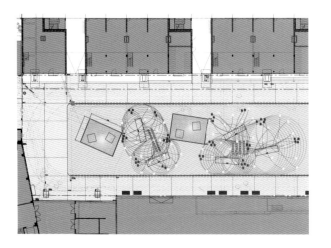

WEISS MANFREDI ARCHITECTS | NEW YORK, USA

Website	www.weissmanfredi.com
Project	Sculpture Park / Urban Waterfront Park
Location	Seattle, USA
Year of completion	2007
Materials	precast concrete, cast-in-place concrete, concrete, steel, glass, riprap rock
Photo credits	Paul Warchol, Weiss Manfredi Architects, Benjamin Benschneider

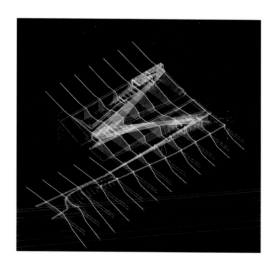

This project has been developed in an area of **Seattle** with a strong post-industrial legacy: 8.9 acres previously occupied by factories. In order to gain ground on the already existing infrastructures (train tracks and four-lane highway), they projected a zigzag walk that connect the urban nucleus with the bay. The sloped planes are reinforced by raised walkways and concrete walls that limit off micro-spaces of autochthonous origin: an evergreen forest with ferns in the undergrowth, another of aspen (Quaking Aspens) and a garden arranged in terraces with halophytic vegetation next to the sea. While walking visitors find sculptures by reputed artists such as Richard Serra, Mark Dion, Calder and Tony Smith, as if the park were a visual continuation of the walls of the 10,170 ft² multi-purpose pavilion located up on top.

Diese Anlage entstand in einem Viertel von Seattle mit betont postindustriellem Charakter. Auf dem 3,6 ha großen Gelände standen einst Fabriken. Um der noch existierenden Infrastruktur Raum abzugewinnen (Gleise, eine vierspurige Straße) wurde eine zickzackförmige Promenade angelegt, die den Stadtkern mit der Bucht verbindet. Die geneigten Ebenen werden durch schwebende Laufstege und Betonmauern gestützt, die die kleinen Flächen mit einheimischer Vegetation begrenzen. Auf einer davon wachsen immergrüne Pflanzen mit Farnkraut im Unterholz, auf einer anderen Zitterpappeln, und schließlich gibt es einen auf Terrassen angelegten Garten mit halophiler Küstenvegetation. Der Weg wird von Skulpturen berühmter Künstler wie Richard Serra, Mark Dion, Calder und Tony Smith gesäumt, so als ob der Park eine visuelle Fortsetzung der Wände des Vielzweckpavillons (3 100 m²) auf der Anhöhe wäre.

El proyecto ha sido desarrollado en un zona de Seattle de fuerte legado postindustrial: 3,6 ha ocupadas anteriormente por fábricas. Para ganar terreno a las infraestructuras aún existentes (vías de tren y carretera de cuatro calzadas de ancho), se proyecta un paseo en zig-zag que conecta el núcleo urbano con la bahía. Los planos inclinados vienen reforzados por pasarelas voladas y muros de hormigón, que delimitan microespacios de origen autóctono: un bosque de hoja perenne con helecho en el sotobosque, otro de álamo temblón (Quaking Aspens) y un jardín dispuesto en terrazas con vegetación halófila al lado del mar. A su paso, el visitante se encuentra con esculturas de reputados artistas como Richard Serra, Mark Dion, Calder y Tony Smith, como si el parque fuera una continuación visual de las paredes del pabellón multiusos (3100 m²) situado a lo alto.

Le projet concerne une zone de Seattle, au fort héritage post-industriel : 3,6 ha occupés autrefois par des usines. Pour utiliser les infrastructures encore existantes (voies de train et route à quatre voies), on a conçu une promenade en zigzag qui relie le centre urbain à la baie. Les plans inclinés sont renforcés par des passerelles aériennes et des murs en béton, qui délimitent les micro espaces d'origine autochtone : un bois à feuilles persistantes, comme la fougère dans le sous-bois, ou le tremble (Quaking Aspens) et un jardin disposé en terrasses, doté d'une végétation halophile, à côté de la mer. En se promenant, le visiteur peut admirer les sculptures d'artistes renommés comme Richard Serra, Mark Dion, Calder et Tony Smith, comme si le parc était la continuation visuelle des murs du pavillon polyvalent (3.100 m²), situé sur les hauteurs.

Il progetto è stato realizzato in una zona di Seattle dal forte carattere industriale: 3,6 ha previamente occupati da fabbriche. Per sfruttare al massimo il terreno, è stato disegnato un viale a zigzag che corre tra le strutture esistenti (ferrovia e strada a quattro corsie) e collega il nucleo urbano con la baia. Le superfici inclinate sono rafforzate da passerelle in aggetto e muri in cemento, che delimitano microspazi di vegetazione autoctona: un bosco di alberi a foglia perenne e sottobosco di felci, un altro di pioppi tremoli e un giardino a terrazze con vegetazione alofila in riva al mare. Al suo passaggio, il visitatore si imbatte in sculture di rinomati artisti, come Richard Serra, Mark Dion, Calder e Tony Smith, quasi che il parco prolungasse visualmente le pareti del padiglione multiuso di 3100 m² situato più in alto.

WEST 8 URBAN DESIGN & LANDSCAPE ARCHITECTURE |
ROTTERDAM, THE NETHERLANDS

Website	www.west8.nl
Project	One North Park
Location	Singapore City, Singapore
Year of completion	2006
Materials	stone and concrete
Photo credits	West 8 Urban Design & Landscape Architecture bv

The design of this green lung in Singapore is yet another element more in Zaha Hadid's master plan for One North, the future technological neighborhood of the city. The park functions as a biological corridor among futuristic looking buildings and tries to establish a nexus between the surrounding neighborhoods. The main esplanade, an ideal place for pedestrians and cyclists, incorporates raised walkways with the aim of lending fluidity to the entire open space. The vegetation combines indigenous species –such as Bougainvillea and other pre-existing plants– with more thematic areas such as Fichus Forest, Blossom Forest and the Frangipani Valley. In Buona Vista Park, which is another of the park's names, water stands out as a recurring element. The maximum expression of such lies in the construction of a 460 ft. high wall used to create a waterfall.

Die Gestaltung dieser grünen Lunge in Singapur geschah im Rahmen eines neuen Bebauungsplans von Zaha Hadid für One North, das künftige Technologieviertel der Stadt. Der Park bildet einen biologischen Korridor zwischen futuristisch wirkenden Gebäuden. Er soll auch als Punkt der Kommunikation für die verschiedenen, umliegenden Viertel dienen. Der Hauptplatz, ein idealer Ort für Fußgänger und Radfahrer, ist mit schwebenden Laufstegen ausgestattet, die den gesamten offenen Raum sehr fließend wirken lassen. Der Platz ist mit einheimischen Pflanzen wie Bougainvillea und anderen bewachsen, die hier bereits vorhanden waren. Zusätzlich gibt es thematische Zonen wie den Ficus Forest, den Blossom Forest und das Frangipani Valley. Das Wasser ist ein immer wiederkehrendes Element im Buona Vista Park, wie er auch genannt wird. Besonders auffallend ist dabei eine 140 Meter lange Wassergardine mit Wasserfall.

El diseño de este pulmón verde en Singapore es un elemento más del master plan de Zaha Hadid para One North, el futuro barrio tecnológico de esta ciudad. El parque se articula como corredor biológico entre edificios de estética futurista, e intenta articular un punto de comunión entre los diferentes barrios circundantes. La explanada principal, lugar ideal para peatones y ciclistas, incorpora pasarelas en voladizo con el objetivo de dar fluidez a todo el espacio abierto. La vegetación combina especies autóctonas –como la Bougainvillea y otras plantas preexistentes– con zonas más temáticas como el Ficus Forest, el Blossom Forest y el Frangipani Valley. El agua destaca como elemento recurrente en Buona Vista Park, otro de los nombres que recibe el parque. El levantamiento de un muro cortina de 140 m con agua en cascada es la máxima expresión de ello.

Le design de ce poumon vert à Singapour est un élément supplémentaire du master plan (plan d'ensemble) de Zaha Hadid pour One North, le futur centre technologique de cette ville. Le parc s'articule autour d'un corridor biologique entre des édifices à l'esthétique futuriste, essayant d'être un point de rencontre entre les différents quartiers environnants. L'esplanade principale, lieu idéal pour piéton et cyclistes, intègre des passerelles en saillie, donnant de la fluidité à tout l'espace ouvert. La végétation associe des espèces autochtones –comme le bougainvillée et autres plantas préexistantes– à des zones plus thématiques comme le « Ficus Forest », le « Blossom Forest » et la « Frangipani Valley ». L'eau s'affiche en élément récurrent du Buona Vista Park, un des autres noms du parc. L'élévation d'un mur rideau de 140 m, avec l'eau qui descend en cascade, en est l'expression la plus forte.

Il disegno di questo polmone verde di Singapore forma parte del master plan di Zaha Hadid per One North, il futuro quartiere tecnologico della città. Il parco è un corridoio verde che si snoda tra edifici dall'estetica futurista e che vuole essere un elemento unificatore per i quartieri vicini. Lo spazio aperto principale, luogo ideale per pedoni e ciclisti, presenta passerelle in aggetto che lo rendono fluido. La vegetazione combina specie autoctone — come la Buganvillea e altre piante già presenti nel luogo — con altre come il Ficus Forest, il Blossom Forest e il Frangipani Valley. L'acqua è un elemento ricorrente nel Buona Vista Park, un altro dei nomi che riceve questo parco; Un muro di 140 m dal quale cade acqua in cascata ne è un perfetto esempio.

ZADE & VILÀ ASSOCIATS | BARCELONA, SPAIN

Project	Wood of Life
Location	Leioa, Spain
Year of completion	2003
Materials	weathering steel, reinforced concrete, pine crust, iroko wood, stainless steel
Photo credits	Maricarmen Vilà i Espino

The search for an open and permeable space as a metaphor for life after death was the philosophy behind this Barcelona studio upon winning the contest –called by the University of the Basque Lands– to construct a 4,265 ft^2 space within the Leioa Campus. The place for keeping the ashes of the dead is not thought of as a cemetery or as a park or pantheon, but as a forest. They rejected closing the space off with a roof, since they didn't want to put limits on the projection of the body towards the infinite. The result is a sculptural project which is seen more as a place than as an object: an open and sublime refuge for souls that are parting.

Die Suche eines offenen und durchlässigen Raums als Metapher auf das Leben nach dem Tod. So definierte das Studio aus Barcelona seine Philosophie, nachdem es eine Ausschreibung der Universität des Baskenlandes für die Gestaltung einer 1300 m^2 großen Fläche des Campus von Leioa gewonnen hatte. Der Ort, an dem die Asche der Toten aufbewahrt wird, wird deshalb nicht als Friedhof, Park oder Pantheon verstanden, sondern als ein Wald. Man verzichtete auf das Überdachen des Raumes, da man keine Grenzen für die Projektion des Körpers zum Unendlichen schaffen wollte. So entstand dieser skulpturale Raum, den man statt als Objekt als einen Ort verstehen muss, ein offener und erhabener Zufluchtsort für die Seelen, die uns verlassen.

La búsqueda de un espacio abierto y permeable como metáfora de vida tras la muerte. Así se postula la filosofía del estudio barcelonés tras ganar el concurso –convocado por la Universidad del País Vasco– para construir un espacio de 1300 m^2 dentro del Campus de Leioa. El lugar donde albergar las cenizas de los muertos no se plantea, pues, ni como un cementerio ni como un parque o panteón, sino como un bosque. Se ha descartado cerrar el espacio con una cubierta, ya que no se deseaba crear límites a la proyección del cuerpo hacia el infinito. El resultado es un proyecto escultórico visto como lugar más que como objeto: un refugio abierto y excelso para las almas que nos dejan.

La quête d'un espace ouvert et perméable, métaphore de la vie après la mort. Telle est la philosophie du bureau d'études barcelonais qui a gagné le concours –lancé par l'Université du Pays Basque– pour la construction d'un espace de 1.300 m^2 au sein du Campus de Leioa. Le lieu qui abrite les cendres des morts n'est pas planté, à l'instar d'un cimetière, d'un parc ou d'un panthéon, mais agencé comme un bois. L'espace n'est pas fermé par une toiture, pour ne pas créer de limites à la projection du corps vers l'infini. Il en résulte un projet sculptural, vu comme un lieu plutôt que comme un objet : un refuge ouvert et exceptionnel pour les âmes qui nous quittent.

Ricerca di uno spazio aperto e permeabile come metafora della vita dopo la morte; questa la filosofia dello studio barcellonese dopo aver vinto il concorso indetto dall'Università dei Paesi Baschi per il progetto di uno spazio di 1300 m^2 nel campus di Leioa. Il luogo dove conservare le ceneri dei defunti non è più un cimitero o un parco o un pantheon, ma bensì, un bosco. Si è deciso di non chiudere lo spazio con una copertura, per non ostacolare la proiezione del corpo verso l'infinito. Ne risulta un progetto plastico, da considerarsi un luogo più che un oggetto: un rifugio aperto e sublime per le anime che ci abbandonano.

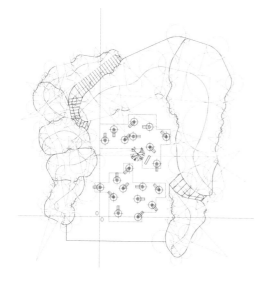

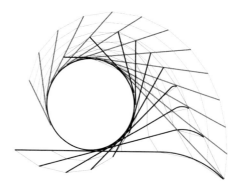

INDEX

Guallart Architects
Puig i Xoriguer 10
08004 Barcelona, Spain
P +34 93 324 86 92
F +34 93 442 73 01
www.guallart.com
Vinaròs Microcoasts
Photos © Nuria Díaz

Gualtiero Oberti
Via degli Assonica 3
24010 Azzonica di Sorisole (BG), Italy
P/F +39 035 573 120
gualtiero.oberti@awn.it
Fluvial Park of Cunella
Photos © Gualtiero Oberti

Gustafson Porter
Linton House 39-51, Highgate Road
London NW5 1RS, UK
P +44 0 207 267 2005
F +44 0 207 485 9203
www.gustafson-porter.com
Diana, Princess of Wales Memorial Fountain
Photos © Helene Binet

Jensen & Skodvin Arkitektkontor AS
Fredensborgveien 11
0177 Oslo, Norway
P +47 22 99 48 99
F +47 22 99 48 88
www.jsa.no
Gudbrandsjuvet Tourist Project
Photos © Jensen & Skodvin Arkitektkontor AS

Karres en Brands Landschapsarchitecten bv
Oude Amersfoortseweg 123
1212 AA Hilversum, The Netherlands
P +31 35 642 29 62
F +31 35 642 13 16
www.karresenbrands.nl
De Nieuwe Ooster Cemetery
Photos © Karres en Brands
Landschapsarchitecten bv, Peter Zoech

Kengo Kuma & Associates
2-24-8 BY-CUBE 2-4F
Minamiaoyama Minato-ku
Tokyo 107-0062, Japan
P +81 03 3401 7721
F +81 03 3401 7778
www.kkaa.co.jp
Chokkura Plaza & Shelter
Photos © Daici Ano

Kristine Jensens Tegnestue
Mejlgade 50 BB ST
DK-8000 Aarhus C, Denmark
P +45 8618 9634
F +45 8618 9633
www.kristinejensen.dk
Prags Boulevard
Photos © Simon Høgsberg, Christina Capetillo

Kuhn Truninger Landschaftsarchitekten GmbH
Ankerstraße 3
8004 Zurich, Switzerland
P +41 44 291 18 19
F +41 44 291 18 20
www.kuhntruninger.ch
Weiach Cemetery
Photos © Ralph Feiner